THE MUSE LEARNS TO WRITE

THE MUSE LEARNS TO WRITE

Reflections on Orality and Literacy from Antiquity to the Present

ERIC A. HAVELOCK

Yale University Press
NEW HAVEN AND LONDON

Library of Congress Cataloging-in-Publication Data

Havelock, Eric Alfred.
    The muse learns to write.

    Bibliography: p.
    Includes index.
    1. Oral communication—History. 2. Written
communication—History. 3. Communication—Greece—History. I. Title.
P90.H38   1986   001.54'2   86–9084
ISBN : 978-0-300-04382-2 (pbk.)

12 11 10 9

*The paper in this book meets the guidelines for permanence
and durability of the Committee on Production Guidelines
for Book Longevity of the Council on Library
Resources.*

Printed in the United States of America

For Christine

Contents

Acknowledgments

Insofar as the oral-literate problem has increasingly become not just a Greek problem but a modern one, readers of the present volume will recognize a debt owed to the work of Walter J. Ong, whose own *Orality and Literacy* (1982), a masterly survey, has provided foundation for the synthesis attempted here. As he has freely acknowledged my usefulness in dealing with Greek antiquity, I also gratefully acknowledge how much I have used him for my dealings with modernity. Closer to home, I owe much to the intellectual support and personal sympathy of John Hollander, whose warm advocacy has been the more welcome as coming from within a department at Yale where the voice of classical antiquity has always been able to count on a sympathetic hearing.

Where my argument has ventured to seek support from the history of archaic Greek art, necessary guidance has been supplied by Christine Havelock.

My manuscript has received close and sympathetic reading from the Yale University Press, in the person of its editor Ellen Graham. Surely, few authors can claim the good fortune of such helpful revision applied to matters not only of detail but of general expression.

My text also owes much to the scrutiny and correction it received from my copyeditor Jay Williams.

E.A.H.
New Milford, Connecticut

1

Program of Investigation

The intention of this book is to present a unified picture of a crisis that occurred in the history of human communication, when Greek orality transformed itself into Greek literacy. Investigations on separate aspects of this problem as I have pursued them in the last thirty-three years lie dispersed in three books and a variety of articles, some only recently published and some now available in foreign translations (see Bibliography). It seems appropriate that their varied conclusions be brought together in a single perspective covering the way in which the transformation took place, what it signified at the time, and what it has since meant for ourselves. Greek literature and Greek philosophy represent twin enterprises of the written word, the first of their kind in the history of our species. Precisely why they were the first, and what precisely constituted their uniqueness, are questions which can best be answered in the context of what has been called the Greek literate revolution.

A hint, but only a hint, that a problem of this kind concerning the character of Greek culture was waiting for explanation first appeared in a book otherwise addressed to a quite different theme. *The Liberal Temper in Greek Politics* (1957) contained the observation that the so-called "fragments" of Democritus did not appear to be quotations extracted from otherwise lost works, but on the contrary were intended by their

1

author to serve as self-contained aphorisms. "The rounded sentence began its career in the pre-literate days of oral communication, when indoctrination depended on word of mouth and retention of doctrine depended on the memory" (Havelock 1957, p. 126).

One scholar (the only one so far as I know) who noted the observation and its possible significance was Arthur Nock, in a personal conversation for which I shall always be grateful. I believe it served to suggest further research on the later use of the philosophic aphorism, which appeared in a valuable article by Zeph Stewart (1958, pp. 179–91).

At the time I refrained from pushing the oralist thesis any further, so far as it concerned the pre-Socratics (but see Hanfmann 1953, p. 24*n*1). I came nearer to doing so in an article on "Parmenides and Odysseus" (1958) in which I probed the philosopher's choice of Homeric themes to guide the composition of his own philosophic poem. Here was a phenomenon which might become fully explicable only within a context of general Greek oralism, still exerting in Parmenides' own day a control over pre-Socratic composition and thought. This prospect was finally opened up in "Preliteracy and the Pre-Socratics" (1966a) in which I brought myself to argue the case for supposing that at least the first four pre-Socratics whose actual language survives composed as oralists either in verse or in aphorisms, in a style which embraced the language of Homer and Hesiod as a matter of course, and that they even accepted the cosmic mythologies of Homer and Hesiod as traditional models which had to be revised. More recently, a treatment of monograph length, "The Linguistic Task of the Pre-Socratics" (1983b), by restricting itself to an examination of all actual pre-Socratic quotations, has been able to draw the conclusion that this "task" should be conceived not as offering rival systems of thought, but as the invention of a conceptual language in which all future systems of philosophic thought could be expressed; this same language, however, being extracted from Homer and Hesiod and given a new non-oralist syntax. The same monograph examined the supposed evidence (supplied by Theophrastus) supporting the view that the Milesian School, so-called (the title was proposed in later antiquity), pioneered in the use of a conceptual vocabulary, with particular reference to the supposed concept of "The Unlimited" (*to apeiron*). The conclusion drawn was that the evidence does not exist; these pioneers, like their successors, composed for oral publication, in oral idiom, and probably in verse.

The primitive theoretic language, which, as I thought I now perceived, was being extracted from Homer and Hesiod and hammered out, was one the pre-Socratics wished to apply to the physical cosmos. The terms sought were primarily physical—body, space, motion, change, quality, quantity, and similar concepts—basic and rather simple (as they appear to us).

What of the moral cosmos, the vocabulary of moral values, the just, the right, the good, the dutiful and the expedient, the obligatory and the permissible? Did these conceptions as expressed in a language of ethics also come into existence only with the written word? Did ethics like physics have to be invented, and did the invention depend upon the substitution of literacy for orality? Obviously, this could be a subversive line of thought, better postponed until some foundation had been laid by dealing with the physical world first.

However, it turned on the same besetting problem of vocabulary change, accompanied by syntactical change, as these became perceptible in the language used to describe human behavior, as against cosmic behavior. My curiosity had originally been aroused by noticing that Plato's term for "justice," a central theme of his best-known work, the *Republic,* was a five syllable word which in that form could not be found in any text earlier than Herodotus. The shorter two syllable form occurred in Homer, Hesiod, and later authors, but never in the kind of syntax assigned to the longer form. Some conclusions that might be drawn from this were indicated in "*Dikaiosune:*

An Essay in Greek Intellectual History" (1969). Not till nearly ten years later were these enlarged in *The Greek Concept of Justice from Its Shadow in Homer to Its Substance in Plato* (1978a). The argument as completed offered the twin proposal that the notion of a moral value system which was autonomous, while at the same time capable of internalization in the individual consciousness, was a literate invention and a Platonic one, for which the Greek enlightenment had laid the groundwork, replacing an oralist sense of "the right thing to do," as a matter of propriety and correct procedure.

My methodology required sticking to the evidence of actual texts rather than loose speculation. This meant leaving out the presence of Socrates in the story, since no Socratic text exists in the sense in which we can say a Platonic text exists. The nearest thing available was a text of a burlesque of the things he was actually saying orally when he was about forty (Plato being a child at the time). How the gap might begin to be filled was indicated in "The Socratic Self as It Is Parodied in Aristophanes' 'Clouds'" (1972).

In fact, this was another instance where a hint of the correct context within which a problem—in this case the Socratic one—might find solution had been thrown out twenty years earlier, in an essay that asked the question "Why Was Socrates Tried?" As part of the answer, I had noted that until the latter half of the fifth century "there were no text-books nor disciplines of law, business management, or agriculture and the like, any more than there were of the arts and crafts. In fact, the processes of a general education had to conform to the conditions of an oral culture" (Havelock 1952, p. 100).

The mechanism, if it can be called such, for maintaining this "education" by guaranteeing its transmission from generation to generation was one typical of an oral society: namely the habit, sedulously cultivated, of close daily association (*sunousia*) between adolescents and their elders who served as "guides, philosophers, and friends" (ibid.). The institution favored homosexual bonding for this purpose. In a male dominated society of extended families, the arrangement enjoyed the firm support of male parents. The offense of Socrates was to propose that in effect this education be professionalised, its context being no longer set by poetic tradition and by practice (*empeiria*) but by dialectical examination of "ideas"—an obvious threat to political and social control hitherto wielded by the leaders of the Athenian "first families."

The Socratic education (*paideusis*) and the Socratic notion of self were thus proposed as missing links in a possible solution of the Socratic problem, both of them raising issues within the context of the oral-literate equation, since a discovery of "selfhood" could be regarded as part and parcel of that separation of the knower from the known which a growing literacy favored (Havelock 1963, chapter 11). The issues raised turned once more on matters of linguistic usage: the vocabulary of education, and the vocabulary of self-realization. Could not the whole Socratic mission be viewed as a linguistic enterprise, propelled by the oral-literate transition? If so, Socrates himself played a paradoxical role, an oralist adhering to the habit of his youth, yet using oralism in a brand new manner, no longer as an exercise in poetic memorization, but as a prosaic instrument for breaking the spell of the poetic tradition, substituting in its place a conceptual vocabulary and syntax, which he as a conservative sought to apply to the conventions governing behavior in an oral society in order to rework them. The dialogues of his disciples, themselves literates of the new generation, carried the results of this innovation to their logical conclusion by writing them out, thereby also extending their interpretation beyond the horizon of the original. Here was revisionism with a vengeance, as applied to the most famous of all philosophic enterprises. The full conclusions that such revisionism may require have only been published in the last two years: "The Socratic Problem: Some Second Thoughts" (1983a) and "The Orality of Socrates and the Literacy of Plato:

With Some Reflections on the Origin of Moral Philosophy in Europe" (1984).

The researches so far accounted for, as they have explored the linguistic effects of a Greek literate revolution, have focused on these as they occurred in the field of Greek philosophy. This indeed was where my initial curiosity had been aroused at a time (1925) when I was specializing in preparation for Division B of Part Two of the Cambridge classical Tripos, which allowed for concentration in the pre-Socratic field. These pre-Socratics (or pre-Platonics, a chronologically more accurate designation which I now prefer, since it correctly puts Socrates in his place close to the oralist period) had been my first love, and have remained so; it is a fascination which I observe to be shared by scholars and philosophers outside the field of classics. For the actual texts of these thinkers, in the Cambridge classroom of those days, we were referred to a textbook (Ritter 1913) in which selected quotations from the originals were intermingled with the interpretative language that had been applied to them in antiquity after they were dead, and very often long after. I observed what I thought to be a collision between the two, in vocabulary and idiom. Ancient interpretations, no less than their modern equivalents, seemed to require that a metalanguage be imposed on the originals. A desire to explain why this was so may be said to have been the starting point for everything I have since published concerning the orality problem in Greece and beyond Greece. For me, this was where it all began, not as is often supposed with Milman Parry's work on Homer (in particular his two articles of 1930, 1932), which I gratefully encountered only fifteen years later.

I had equal reasons for gratitude when Harold Cherniss published *Aristotle's Criticism of Pre-Socratic Philosophy* (1935). This work opened up the whole metalanguage issue by exploring with precision how Aristotle's own physical conceptions had infected his account of pre-Socratic first principles. I was preparing to launch a similar assault on a much wider front, an endeavor that was further encouraged eighteen years later by the appearance of John McDiarmid's *Theophrastus on the Pre-Socratic Causes* (1953). Within a year, the movement toward a reappraisal of the Aristotelean versions of pre-Socratic thought received fresh impetus from the publication of G. S. Kirk's *Heraclitus: The Cosmic Fragments* (1954). This work placed the term *logos* (one with linguistic implications) firmly at the center of the philosopher's system, displacing the elemental fire assigned to him by Aristotle as a first principle. Both McDiarmid and Kirk had previously shared with me at Toronto and Harvard oral discussion centered on these topics.

Extending the perspective set by philosophical language, I began to note the problem, as it seemed to me, of the apparent monopoly exercised by the Muse of poetry over the entire body of early Greek literature. In terms of modernity this was a puzzle. What had happened to the prose which we take for granted in our own culture and which presumably exists in any culture? I re-read the strictures that Plato applies to poetry, in particular to Homer, Hesiod, and Greek drama. Following the party line current in my own subject, I had previously supposed these were not to be taken at face value. Plato did not really mean what he said, or else he said it for only temporary and limited purposes. But suppose he did mean it? What then was his motive? His own chosen language was prose, and elaborately written prose at that. For whatever reason, it had shaken off the previous poetic monopoly. So too, to be sure, had two other writers before him; but Herodotus was an Ionian who wrote in his native dialect, not an Athenian; and Thucydides on his own account began to write only about the time Plato was born, or a little later.

A solution to Plato's strictures, it occurred to me, might lie in the oral-literate equation, so far as it concerned Greek culture as a whole, and this thesis is what I put forward in *Preface to Plato* (1963). The authority provided by the most revered of philosophers was used to explain what had been happening

before him. He was attacking the poets less for their poetry
(one might say) than for the instruction which it had been their
accepted role to provide. They had been the teachers of Greece.
Here was the clue. Greek literature had been poetic because
the poetry had performed a social function, that of preserving
the tradition by which the Greeks lived and instructing them
in it. This could only mean a tradition which was orally taught
and memorized. It was precisely this didactic function and the
authority that went with it to which Plato objected. What
could have been his motive, unless he intended that his own
teachings should supplant it? What was the difference? The
obvious one, already noted, was that his own teaching was
formally nonpoetic. It was composed in prose. Was this a su-
perficial accident? Or, since it represented a replacement for
poetry, was it also meant to replace orality? Was the arrival of
Platonism, meaning the appearance of a large body of discourse
written in prose, a signal announcing that Greek orality was
giving way to Greek literacy and that an oral state of mind was
to be replaced by a literate state of mind? A replacement which
Plato's genius intuitively recognized?

   Preface to Plato suggested that if this was so, then a key role
had been played by the invention of the Greek alphabet, but
the question of exactly how or why was not taken up until I
was afforded an opportunity to do so in "Prologue to Greek
Literacy" (Havelock 1973a). These two discourses dealt respec-
tively with "The Transcription of the Code of a Non-Literate
Culture" and "The Character and Content of the Code." Sub-
sequently, I have seen reason to suspect my own use of the term
code as I had applied it to what I was then talking about (below,
chapter 7).

   The more I thought about the act of transcription as it occurred in Greece, the more convinced I became that there was
something about the Greek writing system which put it in a
class by itself. Its uniqueness could not have been a matter of
simply adding five vowels as though the problem were a sum

in arithmetic. Like many of my generation, raised in the traditions of a more conservative culture, I was familiar with the Old Testament and had begun acquaintance with the so-called "literatures" of Sumer, Babylon, and Assyria (as these have been recently translated from cuneiform tablets) as well as versions of Egyptian wisdom literature. A stark contrast appeared between the sheer richness of Greek orality as transcribed and the caution of its competitors. A wealth of detail and depth of psychological feeling contrasted with an economy of vocabulary and a cautious restriction of sentiment which seemed to be specific properties of all Near Eastern and Hebrew literature. It occurred to me that the true orality of these non-Greek peoples was not getting through to us—had in fact been irretrievably lost, because the writing systems employed were too imperfect to record it adequately. These peoples could not have been stupid, or insensitive, or of a lower order of consciousness. The contrast was pointed up in an article on "The Alphabetisation of Homer" (1978b), which placed portions of comparable texts of the *Epic of Gilgamesh* and the *Iliad* side by side and subjected them to a vocabulary count. A year later ("The Ancient Art of Oral Poetry," 1979) the comparison was extended to include Hindu Vedic literature as an example of ritualized orality, in which simplification may have been encouraged by the limitations of the Sanskrit script in contrast to the scope and detail exhibited in Hesiod's text. Scholars of Hebrew, of cuneiform, of Sanskrit, were not likely to welcome such a thesis, but I had been emboldened to assert it after I had considered some of the acoustics involved in linguistic behavior and had traced the way in which the Greek symbols had succeeded in isolating with economy and precision the elements of linguistic sound and had arranged them in a short atomic table learnable in childhood. The invention for the first time made possible a visual recognition of linguistic phonemes that was both automatic and accurate. The analysis was first offered in *Origins of Western Literacy* (1976), a monograph reprinted in

The Literate Revolution in Greece and Its Cultural Consequences (1982a). Both titles reflect growing awareness that an invention which had proved crucial in changing the character of the Greek consciousness was to do the same thing for Europe as a whole and in fact could be held responsible for creating the character of a modern consciousness which is becoming worldwide. Marshall McLuhan had drawn attention to the psychological and intellectual effects of the printing press: I was prepared to push the whole issue further back, to something that had begun to happen about seven hundred years before Christ.

"Changing the consciousness" is a useful phrase insofar as it invites a critical penetration below the surface level of human life. But it remains loose in application until its truth is tested by demonstrated change in actual linguistic usage, as revealed in the texts of the Greek "authors" we read. Here in their written words (whether or not they themselves did the writing) must be proof or lack of it for the oralist-literate equation.

Philosophic texts, even the texts of Plato, are quantitatively the lesser part of the story. High classic literature is constituted out of a body of poetry composed by the classical masters, Homer, Hesiod, the lyric and choric poets, Pindar, and the three Athenian dramatists.

Preface to Plato, accepting Plato's affirmation of Homer's didactic role as essential to an understanding of the two epics, sought actual examples of didactic content in the first book of the *Iliad* as exhibited in the typicality of scenes and sentiments expressed. A critical reviewer at the time noted the restriction to one book, which might prove nothing about the other twenty-three (Gulley 1964). I had assumed that given the consistency of Homer's style, what was evidently true of one book would in varying degree be true of the others. *The Greek Concept of Justice* provided remedy by offering analysis on similar lines of a few more selected episodes from the *Iliad* and the *Odyssey* (Havelock 1978a, chapter 4). A commentary on the Homeric text that applied the methodology exhaustively might fill several volumes.

Milman Parry, correctly understanding the use of formulas as inspired by conditions of oral composition, assumed that this kind of composition was an art of improvisation. Telling his tale, the singer might be, as we say, "at a loss for words" unless he had readily available, in his memory, a stock of standardized phraseologies from which to select ones that suited a given context in his story. The course of the story would be a matter of invention; the language used for it was not. The model for this conclusion was the observed practice of Yugoslav peasant singers (A. Parry 1971).

Preface to Plato sought to shift attention, so far as the original Greek epics were concerned, away from improvisation toward recollection and remembrance, applied to content as well as style, and on a larger scale of reference, since what was now embraced was the whole tradition of the society for which the bard sang, something which it was his didactic purpose to conserve.

The Greek Concept also took the more drastic step of asserting that since the didactic purpose was to conserve not any tradition but the one governing current society (that is, the one contemporary with the singer) and since the Homeric poems as we have them cannot predate 700 B.C. and can be shown to include materials of an even later date, the traditional way of life celebrated in both poems was that of contemporary Ionia, a community of independent seafaring cities speaking a common language, not that of a fabled Mycenae or any other legendary "source." Mycenae was the suit of clothes in which the tale had to be dressed to give a distance and dignity to certain institutions and attitudes which were contemporary, fulfilling a role rather like that of the Arthur legend in English literature (Havelock 1978a, chapter 5). It was precisely this accent on still contemporary values and attitudes that Plato found objectionable.

Possible implications of this view so far as it might affect Homer's "date" were pushed further in the article cited above on "The Alphabetisation of Homer," which proposed that a later tradition concerning the final composition of the poems, which seems to have been already known by the end of the fifth century B.C. but is now generally dismissed by scholars of the Homeric Question (but see Goold 1960, pp. 272–91; Davison 1962) should be rehabilitated. In its full form (reported by Cicero) this tradition asserted that during the time of Pisistratus in the sixth century the materials of the two epics had been consolidated in some fashion to form the present connected wholes we now have and that this process (or event) occurred in Athens. I drew the conclusion that the process of alphabetization had been slow (a reasonable view on other grounds), that the epics were committed to papyrus piecemeal, and that the organized form in which we now know them was achieved by using the eye as well as the ear.

This judgment reflected a revision of my previously held assumption, forcefully present in *Preface to Plato*, that the two epics, though obviously written down (or we would not have them) were compositions of primary orality: that is, their textual existence and shape represented a faithful rendering of purely acoustic laws of composition as these governed not only style but content. This had always been the contention of firm oralists (Milman Parry, Lord, Kirk) whether or not they were prepared to consider didactic purpose as well. Adam Parry (1966) proposed what in effect was a modification of this position but did not live long enough to enlarge his views further. It had begun to dawn on me that the clues to composition might be more complex (see below, chapter 10).

Such a necessary revision of a previously simplistic view had become predictable from an essay on "The Sophistication of Homer" (1973b) which passed in review two separate sets of episodes in the *Iliad:* the members of each set being closely related to each other, but widely dispersed throughout the twenty-four books. One set described "Comedy on Olympus." Of this I wrote: "The characters are sharply etched, the situation delineated with realism and with nicety, and with an unsparingly ironic eye. Homer is looking at a domestic household with complex relationships, and paints these in with strokes that are sure and swift. The total effect is coherent and also comic." Another set exposed "The Heart of Helen." Of these, I wrote: "Helen, Hector, Paris, and Priam emerge in joint relation only in these three widely scattered contexts. Yet the contexts are not only congruent, they supplement each other with a fine economy. On their first appearance, the poet arranges them in three separate but overlapping pairs: Hector with Paris, Priam with Helen, Helen with Paris. The sixth book follows this up by combining Hector, Paris, and Helen in a trio. In the twenty-fourth, all four are finally brought together within the compass of Helen's last retrospective pronouncement. What kind of genius was it that was capable of such subtleties, operating on the margin of his main plot?" (Havelock 1973b, pp. 267, 275).

This kind of question, I now conclude, can be answered only by accepting that the epics as we now know them are the result of some interlock between the oral and the literate; or, to vary the metaphor, the acoustic flow of language contrived by echo to hold the attention of the ear has been reshuffled into visual patterns created by the thoughtful attention of the eye.

Turning to Hesiod, *Preface to Plato* had examined the poet's account of the Muses' parentage and present performance, concluding that this account strongly supported the view that the purpose of oral poetry, including Homer's, was to contrive a memorized version of social and civic tradition and government (Havelock 1963, chapter 9). The psychology of this oral performance, and the mnemonic purposes it fulfilled, received fresh attention in *The Greek Concept of Justice* drawing from the central roles assigned to song, dance, and melody in the written literature of Greece (Havelock 1978a, chapter 3).

And yet, Hesiod's text is indeed a text, the organization of which again betrays the use of the reading eye, but applied to more sophisticated purposes (albeit less pleasing) than was true in Homer's case. What was being read was Homer himself (not necessarily the epics as completed). Reading him and backward-scanning him, Hesiod was impelled to rearrange him, and so advance the inception (but only that) of a new type of discourse—a "proto-literate" type. The *Greek Concept* put this thesis to the test through a detailed examination of Hesiod's poetic essay on "justice" (*dikē*) which constitutes a significant episode included in the poet's *Works and Days*—significant in this case, because its erratic language could arguably be seen as the result of putting together a series of memories of Homeric contexts that had some associative linkage with the chosen topic; the linkage being of a kind which required support from a previous reading of Homeric texts rather than just remembering them orally (Havelock 1978a, chapters 11 and 12).

The same methodology had been applied earlier to explain the curious construction of a companion episode on the topic of "contention" (*eris*) which Hesiod had used to introduce the same work (Havelock 1966b).

Since Plato's critique of poetry had included tragedy along with epic as the common target of attack, it seemed logical to turn next to the Athenian drama as a possible arena of competition between the oral and the written.

An early play, the *Seven Against Thebes*, offered itself as a suitable subject for analysis, particularly since sixty-two years after its first production it made a re-entry as the subject of a critique in a comedy of Aristophanes, precisely at a time when Athenian orality can be presumed to be yielding to Athenian literacy. "The Oral Composition of Greek Drama" (1980) elicited from the text of the tragedy the evidence that its style of composition responded to oral roles of composition which would assist memorization of a content considered to be socially useful.

Both these traits—the oral style and the didactic purpose—reappear in Aristophanes' comic critique, which by way of contrast also lampoons Euripidean tragedy for its bookishness.

The text of the *Oresteia,* produced nine years after the *Seven,* had already been scrutinized to discover how it managed the symbols of justice (Havelock 1978a, pp. 280–95). It was concluded that their linguistic behavior covered overlapping meanings which verged on contradiction, a manner which could be said to reflect the ad hoc empiricism of orality as opposed to the consistent clarity of literate conceptualism. "It is still the justices of Hesiod that we contemplate, not the justice of Plato" (p. 295).

What of Aeschylus' successors? Were they strictly literate writers, emancipated from the Homeric rule? The *Oedipus Tyrannus* was selected for this test, as par excellence a play of sophisticated composition according to modern literate standards. When all allowance is made for this indisputable quality of the play, the same text yields evidences of the continuing pressure to compose didactically for oral memorization (Havelock 1981).

Both these treatments of Greek drama observed the crucial role played by the choruses in the conservation of current tradition, communicated through the orality of song, dance, and melody. Here were the proprieties of civic behavior, its approved attitudes, its rituals implicit in daily life, re-enacted and recommended over and over again. Such didacticism is carried over implicitly into the dialogue and rhetoric of the characters as they perform the plots. The typicalization previously noted as characteristic of the Homeric narratives lasts on in Greek drama.

Yet the inventions applied to the story line of the plots, together with the growing psychological insights expressed in the stage dialogues, demonstrate that the influence of orality was fading. Ground was being prepared for a technology of the written word, taking shape in a new type of syntax. Plato was to demand that the traditional language of epic and drama be remodeled and replaced by a language of theoretic analysis (Havelock 1978a, pp. 330–34).

In the ground covered by what I have written concerning

the oral-literate equation as it operated in Greece, there are some empty spaces. Pindar is not there, nor the early lyric poets, nor Euripides, or the historians whose methods of managing prose surely offered an alternative, and perhaps a rival, to Plato's own type of discourse. Nor has the ending of the story in Aristotle been reached, if indeed it does end there. The "unified picture" that has been promised will require that these omissions be remedied.

So far, the story has been a Greek one, and in this book it must largely remain so. Its heroine is the Greek Muse, not her modern progeny. She is the voice of a small Mediterranean people as they lived in the three and a half centuries that separate Homer from Aristotle, and as they became involved in the oral-literate equation. Yet the reader will find that after she has been introduced (chapter 2) attention is diverted for a while (chapters 3–7) to concerns lying outside the field of classics and to works of modern scholars and critics with which the Muse herself might not seem to be directly concerned.

The fact is that the oral-literate equation has become no longer just a Greek equation. It has drawn attention, as something still operative in the modern world, from the various disciplines of anthropology, sociology, and comparative literature. Examination of orality's survival in societies which have till recently remained nonliterate has turned into observation of its continuing presence behind the literary texts composed by modern "writers." Current theory may even juxtapose orality and "textuality" in a relationship which appears to be confrontational.

A reading of Jacques Derrida's *De la Grammatologie* (1967) brought me to realize that the oral-literate problem entered the modern European consciousness with Rousseau. His "noble savage" was essentially conceived as an oralist, and remains very much alive in what is now being written about the spoken word and the written text.

The Greek story completely interpreted becomes part of a

wider interpretation existing in the field of comparative literatures outside the classical domain. The same seems to be true in the field of anthropology as demonstrated in the publication of Jack Goody's *Domestication of the Savage Mind* (1977). This seminal work brought indirect support to my own conviction that Greek literacy changed not only the means of communication, but also the shape of the Greek consciousness.

The Greek story is self-contained, yet the crisis in communication which it describes as taking place in antiquity acquires a larger dimension when measured against what appears to be a similar crisis in modernity. Each illuminates the other once a relationship is established between them.

A few have supposed that some such relationship was established in Toronto between myself and Marshall McLuhan (see below, chapter 3) and his mentor Harold Innis (below, chapter 6). I have even been referred to as a member of a "Toronto school" created by these two Canadian thinkers. The reverse is in fact more likely to be the case. After encountering the work of Milman Parry, guided also by a reading of Martin Nilsson's *Homer and Mycenae* (1933; for me still the classic work on the subject), and following those intuitions born of pre-Socratic studies I have previously referred to, I recall giving two or three public lectures at the University of Toronto on the topic of oral composition, and I suspect Innis was one of those who heard them, at a time when he was thinking along similar lines in his own field (Havelock 1982b). Communication that passed between us later, after I had left Toronto for Harvard, leads me to infer this. His influence passed to McLuhan, whose groundbreaking book *The Gutenberg Galaxy* eventually appeared contemporaneously with my own *Preface to Plato*. McLuhan saw at once that there was an unstated partnership between these two works, and later continued to acknowledge it with a generosity for which I shall always be grateful.

The classical scholar, given the strenuousness of the mental gymnastics required to master Greek and Latin before he can begin to consider things the languages may be talking about, is not likely to stray too far from his subject in pursuit of strange gods on the outside who might have something relevant to say. It was only after reading Walter Ong's *Orality and Literacy* (1982) that I became fully aware of the amount of scholarship and speculation on this subject which had come into existence in the last two decades. The chronological coincidence of five relevant works appearing in 1962–63 (one of them my own) and its possible significance is noted below in chapter 3.

The reader will realize how slowly over the years I have brought myself to write out the various conclusions put together in this volume. I suppose I was teaching them from time to time before I wrote them, and I shall always be grateful for the willingness to listen on the part of students at Toronto, Harvard, and Yale who had minds of their own. Within the context of classical scholarship as traditionally pursued these conclusions will, I suppose, appear revisionist, controversial, and to some even objectionable. There are some natural reasons for this, mostly traditional ones, and I have even thought fit to indicate briefly, in chapter 11, what these may be. They were enough to inspire caution and cause hesitation in publishing them to the point where I am still finishing this book in my eighty-third year. Judging from some things that have been said about them by reviewers, and still more from the evident hope of many scholars that they can be safely ignored, caution has been justified. One place where they were welcomed was in a masterly review of the history of the Homeric Question published by Adam Parry in the year of his premature death as an introduction to the collected edition of his father's works (A. Parry 1971). It is fitting that I remember him here and what he wrote.

2

Introducing the Muse

The history of European literature begins with the poems of Homer and Hesiod. In written form, "Homer" may have made a partial appearance in the early part of the seventh century B.C. Even this vague date is not authenticated; it cannot be checked from any external source. It depends on an inference from the probable date of the invention of the Greek alphabet in which the poems were written. If later tradition is to be believed, they did not achieve the final form in which they have survived to this day until as late as the middle of the sixth century B.C.

As written, there is no previous recorded preparation for them. Virgil, Dante, Milton had their predecessors. They belong in a literary tradition, not narrowly epic, but general. They have genius, but it is not unaided, not unique, not isolated. But the *Iliad* and *Odyssey*—and we must add Hesiod's *Theogony* and *Works and Days*—have no ancestry, no tradition.

But somehow they came to be "written" or "written down" (scholars still dispute which is the right way to describe the "creative act") first either on parchment (not very likely but possible) or on papyrus sheets, gummed together, then rolled up on a stick or cylinder, painfully copied by hand century after century, sheet after sheet, till at last, after Gutenberg, they reached the security of print. What wonder if this historical process, a textual process, has wedded so many scholars to

19

the conviction that these are "literary" works in the fullest
modern sense of the term, composed by "authors" who must
themselves have been "writers."

What then of "authorship"? Can the works themselves yield
any clues to the personalities involved? Surely as poets of first
rank they had colleagues, teachers, models, sources. We do not
know. Even the two names "Homer" and "Hesiod" are
shrouded in uncertainty. One of them, "Hesiod," occurs once
in one of the four poems, in the third person. "[The Muses]
once taught Hesiod glorious song, as he was shepherding
lambs below holy Helicon." The next hexameter employs the
first person: "Speech did the goddesses address to me first of
all, as follows. . . ." Are "Hesiod" and "me" to be equated?
Are they the same person? It is impossible to be quite sure.
Perhaps the naming of the name is a kind of signature, meant
as a hallmark of authorship. Homer (whether one or several)
never identifies himself. Responsibility for the composition of
both *Iliad* and *Odyssey* is assigned to the Muse, who is invited
to "sing" the *Iliad,* "recite" the *Odyssey.* More explicitly, "Hesiod" describes the "song" (not "my song") as something "they
taught."

The author later called Homer, whoever he should be, issues
his invitation in the imperative mood. So he is there, but as
performer, not as author. He mediates between the Muse,
whoever she is, and the audience, as though his verses were not
his own, but derived from a source external to himself, a source
which he called "Muse" and which, we learn from "Hesiod,"
was really a composite of nine sisters (a choir?) who were
daughters of Zeus—this gave them Olympian prestige—and
their mother "Remembrance" (*Mnemosune*). Surely here is a
clue—the first—to the original composition of these four
poems. Nowhere in any of the four is there any hint of interest
in "writing" or "reading" either on the part of the singer or on
the part of the Muse or Muses. The *Theogony,* the poem which
narrates their names and parentage, is introduced by an ex-

tended hymn, in three parts, addressed to all nine and celebrating what they do and what they produce. Repeatedly, in
variant versions, the language they compose is described in
oral terms, as elocution or song, performed while they dance,
and extending acoustically over space to a listening audience.

> They make their fair lovely dances upon highest Helicon
> and move with vigorous feet. Thence they arise and go
> abroad by night veiled in thick mist and utter their
> song with lovely voice. . . .

> Unwearying flows the sweet sound from their lips and
> the house of their father Zeus the loud thunderer is glad
> at the lily-like voice of the goddesses as it spreads
> abroad, and the peaks of snowy Olympus resound and
> the homes of the immortals. . . .

> Then went they to Olympus delighting in their sweet
> voice, with heavenly song, and the dark earth resounded
> about them as they chanted. . . .
>
> [*Theogony*, ll. 7–14, 39–43, 68–70; Loeb translation]

Two centuries later, times have changed. The Muse herself
(or Muses) portrayed on pottery still sings, or at least recites,
but what is really happening is much more complicated. The
texts of the Greek plays we have, both tragic and comic, carry
many signals of an important historical fact. Singing, recitation, and memorization on the one hand (a cultural combina-
tion we can conveniently label as orality) and reading and writing on the other (the habit of a documented and literate
culture) were coming into competition and collision. Not that
the latter was automatically replacing the former. The affair
conducted between them was more subtle; out of scores of examples let us select one, a play produced by Euripides (his
Hippolytus) in 428 B.C. The plot turns on the composition in
writing of a message left by a deceased wife incriminating
(falsely) her stepson. The presence of the tablet on which it is

written is effectively dramatized, lying on the breast of the corpse. The husband arriving home discovers his bereavement, unties the tablet, and reads it to himself on stage. Presumably by this time a theater audience could accept the fact as normal that a woman could write and a man could read. But as he reads, he exclaims spontaneously, "The tablet shouts, it cries aloud. Look, look at what I have seen in written letters (*en graphais*)—a song speaking aloud!" (ll. 877–880).

Logically, if the message is a song or verse sung aloud, you don't see it. If on the other hand it is a written document, it can't sing to you. But the logic of either/or does not belong in these words. They open a window on a cultural process of transition, in which collision and contradiction are of the essence. The Muse of orality, a singer, reciter, memorizer, is learning to read and write—but at the same time she also continues to sing (for these "paradoxes" see Segal 1986, p. 219, who appropriately cites Knox 1968).

Moreover, the recent technique of communicating by written word still suffers some stigma. It is a newcomer. What has been falsely written cannot now be challenged by the truth of traditional oral testimony extracted from witnesses by oral examination. Hippolytus, victim of the accusation, argues this point with vehemence. He fiercely reproaches his father for preferring the written word to the oral—his own included (for the same rule surviving in medieval England, see Clanchy 1979, p. 211). As for the vital oral testimony that could have been extracted from the culprit, that alas is no longer available. She has guaranteed its absence by her suicide (l. 972). Euripides' dialogue hews faithfully to the line required by the complex ethos—the oral-written ethos—of his society and his time.

What has been called the "Literate Revolution" (Havelock 1982a) in Greece is not one more programmed concept conjured out of the air. It is a theory which, as in the instance just cited, uncovers and explains meanings concealed in a thousand passages of classic Greek literature from Homer to Aristotle. It explains what Charles Segal has called the curious "dynamism," never since duplicated, of the high classic Greek vocabulary and syntax. It explains the Greek invention of philosophy. The word *revolution,* though convenient and fashionable, is one that can mislead if it is used to suggest the clear-cut substitution of one means of communication by another. The Muse never became the discarded mistress of Greece. She learned to write and read while still continuing to sing. The following pages seek to describe how this came about.

But first, before she is allowed to take her place on center stage, it is pertinent to cast an eye on what has been going on in the wings. The orality-literacy problem as it concerns the Greeks is not a narrowly technical problem. The perspective within which it is being raised enlarges itself beyond the boundaries of antiquity, for the problem has become a matter of investigation in modern fields of endeavor, ranging from comparative literature to cultural anthropology to biblical studies. Certain forces are at work which seem to be pushing it up to the level of conscious recognition, forcing us to take a look at ourselves on the one hand as writers and readers, yet on the other as performers and listeners, a role which is being revived for us, one might say thrust upon us, by new technologies of communication. Before coming to the Greek story, it may seem fitting to review that modern context within which the story is emerging.

3

The Modern Discovery of Orality

The "Orality Problem," as it has presented itself for investigation during the last twenty-five years, has been argued from several points of view. There is the historical dimension: What has it meant for societies and their cultures in the past to discard oral means of communication in favor of literate ones of various sorts? There is the contemporary one: What precisely is the relationship between the spoken word of today (or yesterday) and the written text? There is the linguistic one: What happens to the structure of a spoken language when it becomes a written artifact? Does anything happen? From this, one can proceed to the philosophical (or psychological) level and ask: Is oral communication the instrument of an oral state of mind, a type of consciousness quite different from the literate state of mind?

A stellar argument conducted overall on these various fronts has erupted during the last two decades within the Western intellectual community with astonishing suddenness and surprising intensity. The year 1963 provides a convenient watershed date: or perhaps better a date when a dam in the modern consciousness appears to burst, releasing a flood of startled recognitions of a host of related facts. To be sure, some notice of the role of the spoken as opposed to the written tongue goes back to the eighteenth century, and more recently field anthropologists have compiled extensive reports of "primitive" societies (meaning nonliterate ones) which have indirectly pointed to the need for a category of human communication designated as primary orality. But the suggestion took the form of a firm concept only after 1963. Walter Ong's *Orality and Literacy* (1982), in which the concept is crystallized and defined, appends a bibliography covering the history of scholarship and speculation in this field, from the eighteenth century to the present. The list of authors and works cited can be conveniently divided chronologically, between those who have written later than 1963 and those who wrote before that date: the later group (excluding those with only peripheral connection to the problem) number 136; the earlier one, 25. Even if one allows for previous works now forgotten and so omitted (if such exist) the disparity is startling.

What, if anything, had happened on or about the year 1963 to precipitate this sudden explosion of interest? An event had indeed occurred, or rather a concurrence of five separate events, in the field of letters and learning—events that in retrospect take on the lineaments of a single phenomenon unperceived at the time, but marking a crisis in the slow realization of the oral problem.

Within the span of twelve months or less, from some time in 1962 to the spring of 1963, in three different countries—France, Britain, and the United States—there issued from the printing presses five publications by five authors who at the time when they wrote could not have been aware of any mutual relationship. The works in question were *La Pensée Sauvage* (Lévi-Strauss), "The Consequences of Literacy" (Goody and Watt, an extended article), *The Gutenberg Galaxy* (McLuhan), *Animal Species and Evolution* (Mayr), and *Preface to Plato* (Havelock).

The titles suggest diversity rather than connection. Yet all five in retrospect can be seen as shedding light often unwittingly upon the role of orality in the history of human culture, and its relation to literacy.

The Mayr volume (whose inclusion may surprise many) comprised an analytic survey and summation of Darwinian evolution as it has been refined and supplemented in its modern sophisticated form. The work has become a classic in its field. Dealing with human culture only as an appendix to biological evolution it pointed to language as the key to the specific humanity of our species (Mayr 1963, pp. 634–37). What it further had to say about the cultural purpose served by language, though crucial to a full understanding of the role of orality in culture, will here be postponed for later consideration.

Of the other four publications, one may be said to have touched on the issue of orality and then backed away from it. The selection of *La Pensée Sauvage* (Lévi-Strauss 1962) from among the author's numerous works, dating before and after, that have expounded the structuralist theory of myth may seem arbitrary until it is remembered that this book appeared prior to the more extensive *Mythologiques* (1964, 1966, 1968) and undertook to establish a relationship—a correspondence one might say—between the structuralist logic of tribal myth (already expounded in *Anthropologie Structurale,* 1958) and contemporary spoken language, particularly in reference to the naming of names (a factor of crucial importance in oralism). Not that the author himself identified the theme of orality latent in this comparison. But it is there, not only latent but laden with future power. If the possible significance of this fact was not exploited, it can be said that the structuralist school was in effect inhibited from exploiting it. That binary arrangement of paired symbols complementing each other which was to be observed latent in all true "myth" had become perceptible as the myths were transcribed; that is, as they became evident in texts. This has meant that for the structuralists it has been difficult to recognize the boundaries dividing oral from written as a subject for formal definition.

In *The Gutenberg Galaxy* (McLuhan 1963) the oral question

is again posed indirectly. The reader can hear it as a muffled echo. McLuhan's text focused not on "primary orality" as it has now been identified but on the cultural transformation which he discerned as occurring upon the invention of printing by moveable types. This, he argued, split the history of human culture between script, which was pre-Gutenberg, and text, which was post-Gutenberg, and fastened on the (presumably) European mind a print mode of consciousness which by implication he saw as constricted and (though he is ambiguous here) regressive. This negative valuation placed on print was sharpened by focusing attention on the modern media, in particular radio. The term "electronics" haunts his pages, as any reader soon discovers. The technology of electronics, so thoroughly acoustic, he argued, reintroduced a nonlinear and richer form of communication and so perhaps of experience, reviving forms that had existed, he implied, before human communication had felt the deadening hand of print.

The book, despite its popular style, performed two services of great importance. It asserted, and largely demonstrated from examples, the fact that technologies of communication as they vary exercise a large measure of control over the content of what is communicated ("The medium is the message"). It also posed, even if indirectly, the question: Does the human mind, or consciousness, or however we may choose to describe it, represent a constant in human history, or has it been subject to historical change? More simply, did human beings once think differently from the way we do now, and do we now think differently from the way we may think in the future? From the first question it was possible to deduce, though the deduction was avoided, that an "oral literature," if the paradox be allowed, would be qualitatively different from a "literate" literature; and from the second, that behind the "linear" consciousness of modernity, derived from the linearity of typography, could be discerned an oral consciousness which follows its own distinct rules of thinking and feeling, existing in a historical past, but now being revived through modern technology in the historical present. These were only implications now seen in retrospect to be latent in this pioneering work, which however preferred to focus on a moment of cultural crisis in the history of modern Europe (hence, the "Gutenberg" in the title) and saw it as having effects both psychological (a shift in the ratio of the senses) and social (the role and rule of the printed book) which were complex and interrelated (hence the "Galaxy").

"The Consequences of Literacy," by Goody and Watt, switched attention to orality as such, and in effect supported the case for a major qualitative difference between orality and literacy. The starting points of their joint conclusions were empirical. Watt, taken prisoner by the Japanese after the fall of Singapore, had been forced to live or, more properly, survive for several years in a society deprived of reading matter, a preliterate society artificially created. Goody, on field trips to Africa, had made contact with tribal groups that were nonliterate, and he had recorded their language and observed their social behavior. To be sure, orality in this African case was somewhat qualified by contact with Moslem culture. But the paper as jointly constructed produced some compelling insights into what a condition of primary orality may be like and the kind of language that is employed in it, and what happens to it on the impact of literacy.

The paper had a double focus. It directed attention toward survival of orality in the modern world, and to a possible model for orality in its relationship to literacy in the experience of ancient Greece. In this area Watt called attention to perhaps three crucial factors: the essential role of personal memory in maintaining the continuity of an oral culture; the formal distinction to be drawn even if tentatively between the Greek alphabet and its immediate predecessors, the Semitic scripts from which it had borrowed; the qualitative difference of the literature and philosophy written in the Greek alphabet when compared with previous so-called literatures (Watt 1962, pp. 319–32).

So far as the role of Greece was considered, Watt's conclusions found correspondence in *Preface to Plato,* but now supported by an intensive examination of the testimonies supplied by some original Greek texts, in particular Plato at the lower end of the historical spectrum and Homer at the other. Plato's rejection of poetry and, in particular, Homer as a proper resource for Greek education (Havelock 1963, chapter 1) was compared with the traditional function of poetry as it had been described earlier in Hesiod (ibid., chapter 6) and with the actual content of Homer's poems (ibid., chapter 4). Plato's acceptance of the didactic function as the main one was demonstrated to be substantially correct. This function was then ascribed to the cultural role of versified language in a society of oral communication, in which effective memorization depended on the use of rhythm. Acting as a kind of versified encyclopedia, Homer recorded and preserved the means of maintaining cultural continuity by putting on record the social mores of the culture (ibid., chapters 3, 4). The support of epigraphy (ibid., pp. 49–52) was sought to draw the conclusion that Greek society in Homer's day had indeed been wholly oral; Homer was not an oral survival in an otherwise literate milieu; this society became literate only by slow degrees in the centuries separating Homer from Plato. Platonism, being a written text, was able to formulate a new conceptual type of language and of thinking as a replacement for oral narrative and oral thinking (ibid., chapters 11–15). Narrative along with rhythm had been the necessary means of supporting the oral memory and was now no longer needed. Finally, the suggestion (but only a suggestion) was offered that clues to the Greek achievement of literacy and the literate state of mind could be discerned in a superior phonetic efficiency of the Greek writing system (ibid., p. 129).

4

Radio & the Rediscovery of Rhetoric

Why, one may ask, should five such works produced simultaneously in three different countries have all involved themselves in the role of human language in human culture? Why, in particular, this focus on the spoken language in contrast to the written? Perhaps the coincidence should not be overdrawn. An ancestry can be traced for such a line of inquiry conducted during the history of modern Europe, going back at least as far as Rousseau. In the field of classical scholarship the orality of Homer, the archetypal poet of the West, had already been examined with some startling results. Yet I think a nerve had been touched common to all of us, an acoustic nerve and so an oral nerve, something that had been going on for over forty years since the end of World War I, to the point where it demanded response. McLuhan's book came nearest to realizing what this experience was, one shared by the writer and the thinker and the scholar and the common man alike. We had all been listening to the radio, a voice of incessant utterance, orally communicating fact and intention and persuasion, borne on the airwaves to our ears. Here was a new type of demand on our attention, even a new force exercised over our minds. It may have been a realization of this force as both a personal and a social thing operating in the politics of our century, aside from any scholarly interest in the subject, that has come to a head in the last two decades, provoking an awareness of tensions set up between the spoken word and the written and of a possible historical origin for this in the experience of the Greeks. *Preface to Plato* even went so far as to compare the antique Greek poetry to a "live recording."

At the present time of writing, since the five works under review appeared, twenty-three years have passed. As already noted, they have witnessed an outpouring, a veritable flood of investigations, in which contact has been sought with the oral-literate problem from a variety of standpoints and in a variety of professional departments. Surely here is a phenomenon of our times peculiar to itself which responds to some deep contemporary experience of a control over audience now extended beyond the expectations of any previous oratory.

The limits of the powers of the human voice from time immemorial had been set by the size of an audience physically present. These were now simply removed. A single voice addressing a single audience on a single occasion could at least theoretically address the entire population of the earth. The potential of the oral spell had been reasserted after a long sleep that had set in perhaps about the time McLuhan said it had, perhaps earlier, perhaps later. As we now probe orality in history we are probing its partial resurrection in ourselves.

Two political personalities totally opposed in temperament and values but both masters of myth-making played a key role in ushering in the new dimension of the spoken word. In their day Franklin Roosevelt and Adolph Hitler embodied power and persuasion over men's minds which was electronically transmitted and which proved functionally essential to the kind of political influence that they wielded. Their prototypes were the minstrels and reciters of the oral ages of the past, but their oral power now extended beyond the range of any previously imagined eloquence. Was this a case of quantitative change turning into a qualitative one?

A personal recollection is relevant. At some time in October of 1939 (I think it was then, soon after Hitler had completed his conquest of Poland, but memory is uncertain) I recall standing on Charles Street in Toronto adjacent to Victoria College, listening to an open air radio address. We all, professors and students, as by common consent had trooped out to listen to the loudspeaker set up in the street. It was broadcasting a speech from Hitler, with whom we in Canada were, formally speaking, at war. He was exhorting us to call it quits and leave him in possession of what he had seized. The strident, vehement, staccato sentences clanged out and reverberated and chased each other along, series after series, flooding over us, battering us, half drowning us, and yet kept us rooted there listening to a foreign tongue which we somehow could nevertheless imagine that we understood. This oral spell had been transmitted in the twinkling of an eye, across thousands of miles, had been automatically picked up and amplified and poured over us. I have sometimes wondered whether McLuhan as a young man in Toronto at that time would have heard the same speech, shared the same experience. Much that he was later to write reflects such a possibility.

I would hazard the guess that Lévi-Strauss might have listened to those accents on the air. He was in the French army. His field work in Brazil was behind him. None of his intellectual engagement with myth was written. Did he sense then a revival of a mythology of the spoken word? Reshaped, manufactured, manipulated, organized by the electronic media? Could one guess that Ian Watt, a prisoner of war in the jungles of Burma a short time later, would have come under a comparable spell through the camp transmitter, his only link with the outside world, his only guarantee of that world's existence? Here was the moving mouth, the resonant ear, and nothing more, our servants, or our masters; never the quiet hand, the reflective eye. Here was orality indeed reborn.

The electronic media to which we have attended ever since World War I have not, however, returned us to that primary orality and they never could. Beside and below the acoustic message there still lurks the written message. To be sure Hitler's oratory was in part a work of improvisation. It was genuinely oral. But it used some previous written preparation, and there was usually a printed supplement that made it available to respond to after the speech was over, one which performed the function of placing it in memory, however temporary. The technology itself which broadcast it was the child of the alphabet, of literacy, of documented definitions, of printed manuals of procedure.

What had happened was not a reversion to a primeval past but a forced marriage, or remarriage, between the resources of the written word and of the spoken, a marriage of a sort which has reinforced the latent energies of both parties. The acoustic media whether in radio or television or on recorded disc or tape cannot possibly carry the sole or even the main burden of communication in the modern world. In fact, a case could be made for the proposition that the technology which has revived the use of the ear has at the same time reinforced the power of the eye and of the written word as it is seen and read. It is here that one must mark the limits of McLuhan's perception of what had been happening. Throughout his work there runs a vein of mysticism, or at least of romantic nostalgia for the directness, the fluidity, the sincerity, the comprehensiveness of a system of communication of ideas which had to yield to the more constricting limits laid upon it by the Gutenberg invention. The oral-literate equation is not that simple.

5

Cross-Cultural Collisions

One of the difficulties of thinking about language is that you have to use language to think about it. A linguistic act has to be directed upon itself. Once written down the act could be visualized and this visual thing could be separated from the act of speaking and laid out in a kind of visual map. But what was the nature and significance of the speaking act itself? What has been its role in man's history?

The impulse to think about the difference between the spoken and written word, and the possibly complex relationship between them, needed a trigger. This was supplied by a special kind of experience, provoked by encountering a cultural collision between the oral act and the writing act. In our day this has occurred between electronic sound and printed word, that is, between hearing something and reading something. Our technological culture has created the collision within itself. As long as reading was the standard operation performed by all people who were thinking intensively, or thought they were thinking, there was little inclination to wonder whether oral thinking might be a bit different from textual thinking.

But besides the counterculture within ourselves, there have been, and in vestigial form may still exist, countercultures outside ourselves altogether. Recognition of these, and of the fact that they might really be viewed as competing cultures, goes back at least as early as the eighteenth century—and in particular to the speculations of Jean-Jacques Rousseau. The discovery of the New World had proved not to be a merely geographic enterprise. It has disclosed to the consciousness of the Old World the existence of tribal societies conducted after a pattern which, it was supposed, Europe from the time of Greece had left behind. The *Voyages* of Hakluyt were first published in 1589 and 1598, those of Captain Cook in 1774 and 1784. *Robinson Crusoe* appeared in 1719, an epic of survival of a literate European under strictly oral conditions. From early in the sixteenth century analogous reports brought back by Spanish and French conquerors and explorers from the New World had also multiplied. The earliest had begun to appear only two decades after Columbus (Bernal Diaz del Castillo 1983). Were the American Indians, the Aztecs and Incas, and the Polynesians, whose existence was now revealed in total cultural independence from Europe, to be viewed as peoples who lived, or had lived, in some sort of civil society? Were they "savage" on the one hand, and yet "noble" on the other, possessors of an ethical simplicity, a direct feeling, which Europeans had lost? And, lurking behind these questions, barely recognized, lay another question. Were they literate or nonliterate? Could they read and write? If not, what comparative value does this negative fact place on writing, in the history of our species, what positive value on its absence? Such theoretical questions, lying beyond the range of interest of the explorers and conquerors, began to be asked by the savants, and provoked their speculations.

A cross-cultural collision had occurred, in the first instance, personal and social, as the firearms of the invaders confronted the bows and arrows of the invaded; in the second instance ideological, as it occurred in the consciousness of European intellectuals, arousing a recognition of their own use of alphabetic writing, so long taken for granted as a natural and native human faculty, albeit relying on education. Was it not only an acquired discipline, but possibly a misfortune, even a "catastrophe"?

Rousseau's *Essay on the Origin of Languages* seems to have appeared between 1754 and 1762 (Derrida 1967, p. 194). It included a chapter "On Script" and a chapter on "Whether it is likely that Homer knew how to write." Both form a kind of appendix to what was central to his interest, an exposition of the existence of a "natural" language, a speech of the passions as opposed to reason, available to the "savages" of his imagination. As his countryman Derrida has noted, Rousseau's attitude to writing is confused, ambiguous, even contradictory. Is it an "enslavement" of the natural spirit of man, or merely a neutral reporter and reflector of the various stages of man's departure from nature? Rousseau perhaps could not make up his mind about this. But the romantic and extravagant value he placed upon "natural," that is "savage" speech (which today we would interpret as strictly "oral" speech), repeated throughout his numerous works, has had a profound influence up to our own day, upon Lévi-Strauss and McLuhan and finally Derrida, whose *De la Grammatologie* appeared in 1967, four years after that watershed conjunction of five works of 1962–63 already noted. Lévi-Strauss in fact set out to endow the "savage mind" of Rousseau with a basic "primitive" habit of structuration. Rousseau did not identify the "oral question" and "orality" as such. A collision between orality and textuality lay beyond his purview. But he laid a foundation for its recognition in our century.

He also anticipated one important element which since 1928 has assisted this recognition. The concept of orality as defining a cultural situation quite distinct from literacy, and using a language of its own, has inevitably drawn support from what has come to be known as the Parry-Lord thesis concerning the oral composition of the Homeric poems. Homer does indeed constitute a crux in the oral problem. It is of direct interest in this connection that Rousseau, who like his contemporaries received some education in the classics, turned his attention to Homer, arguing that the *Iliad* and *Odyssey* could not have been works of writing, though this insight stopped short of any examination of how precisely they could have been composed. Such a question had to wait 150 years for its answer to be supplied by Milman Parry.

The "orality question," then, from its inception in modern times, has been entangled with the "Greek question." Somewhere there, back in classical antiquity, sometime in the first millennium B.C., answers might lurk which would go beyond what can be inferred from "primitive" or "backward" cultures, whether American Indian or Polynesian or, more recently, Yugoslavian and African. But even this backward glance at Greece was originally provoked by experience of a cultural clash born of modernity as it encountered what seemed to be its past, still surviving beyond the Atlantic.

Rousseau's eighteenth-century successor in exploration of the Homeric Question was the Englishman Robert Wood. In classical scholarship this is where the history of the Homeric problem usually begins, before its custody is transferred to the care of German philology, in the person of F. A. Wolf. Wood was a diplomat, traveler, and amateur archaeologist, a pioneer in his day. He traveled extensively in the Mediterranean and the Middle East, tracing what he thought to be the locations of Homer's stories, but more to the point he proposed that "Homer" was a work of the memory, not of writing, and was also a work of "Nature." It is difficult to resist the conclusion that he had read (or encountered?) Rousseau. (Five years had probably elapsed since the final revised appearance of the *Essay*.) However that may be, it is surely not speculative that in the insights he produced the effect of a cultural clash, mediated by his travels, is again at work, this time not with America but with the peasantry of the Middle East. "In a rude and unlettered society, the memory is loaded with nothing that is either useless or unintelligible" (quoted in A. Parry 1971, p. xiii).

For the next hundred years, the written word, increasingly dominant as European mass literacy advanced under liberal or democratic governments, became the sole context within which problems of consciousness and communication were considered. If you did not write and read you were, culturally speaking, a nonperson. The next instance of objectivity provoked by the orality/literacy collision appeared when Malinowski published "The Problem of Meaning in Primitive Languages" (1923). Like Wood, and unlike Rousseau who relied on hearsay reports, the author as a professional anthropologist had made actual contact with pre-literate societies and made the interesting observation, pregnant for later studies, that among "primitive" peoples generally language is a "mode of action"—"though he had trouble explaining what he was getting at" (Ong 1982, p. 32). The term "primitive" by its pejorative sense masked an unwillingness to recognize orality as a formative social process (nor has this ideological playing down been confined to Malinowski). The force of collision had been felt through contact with Polynesia. It is interesting to note that Lévi-Strauss (1936), encountering a similar experience through contact with South American Indians, refused to recognize it as a collision but rather preferred to seek common ground between the oral past and the literate present.

Four years earlier the opportunity for a similar collision with "primitives" (so-called) had occurred on the other side of the world, when Alexander Luria spent two years in intensive observation of nonliterates in the Soviet Republics of Uzbekistan and Kirghizia (Luria 1976). No later investigator ever approached in depth the conclusions he was able to draw, particularly since he took care to make comparison with literates in the same community. His nonliterates, who one gathers were the majority, identified geometrical figures by giving them the names of concrete objects with associated shapes: a circle would be called a plate, sieve, bucket, or watch; school students (on the other hand), moderately literate, identified geometrical figures by their proper categories (reported in Ong 1982, p.

51). Confronted with such a list as hammer, saw, log, hatchet, the nonliterate did not think to classify the log apart from the three tools. All four were granted similar status as belonging to the same situation. "'They all look alike,' says an illiterate peasant: 'the saw will saw the log and the hatchet will chop it'" (ibid.).

> In brief, his illiterate subjects seemed not to operate with formal deductive procedures at all—which is not the same as to say they could not think or that their thinking was not governed by logic but only that they would not fit their thinking in purely logical forms which they seemed to have found uninteresting.
>
> [Ong 1982, p. 52]

This way of putting it still assigns a capacity for "logic" to illiterates, while appreciating the fact that this does not mean "purely logical forms." A more radical question would be to ask: May not all logical thinking as commonly understood be a product of Greek alphabetic literacy?

If Luria discerned total absence of categorical thinking in the nonliterates, did he in his investigation discern a clue to an alternative mode of making meaningful connection between statements? Apparently he did, by choosing as one of his subjects a literate journalist who had the freakish capacity for total recall of lists of objects and their names; in short, a professional mnemonist, which is what he became (Luria 1968). What Luria found was that disconnected names in a long list were memorized by being made to represent actors in a narrative context:

> During these test sessions, S would sit with his eyes closed, then comment "yes, yes . . . this was a series you gave me once when we were in your apartment . . . you were sitting at the table and I in the rocking chair . . . you were wearing a grey suit and you looked at me

like this . . . now then I can see you saying. . . ." And
with that he would reel off the series precisely as I had
given it to him at the earlier session.

[Harding 1968]

This report makes clear that the mnemonic trigger
for repeating the list had to be a narrative situation,
a little story within which the list is embedded, but the
list itself is also retained in narrative form: when S
memorized a list of nouns he needed a few seconds pause
after each item. This gave S time to get a visual image
of the object and set it at a particular point in an imagined background, commonly at intervals along a familiar
street. Once that was done he could just walk along the
street from either end or start from any point en route
and report the things he had placed there.

[Havelock 1978a, p. 44]

This activist narrative of behavior in a connected story was
what the memory preferred to be able to recall, in order to
contain within it a report of the specific items. Whether or not
Luria realized its importance, here was a vital clue to the mode
of operation of the memory that Robert Wood had noted as
unique to oral societies. Its survival is perceptible in Homer.

The complete publication of Luria's investigations in their
original Russian did not occur until well over forty years after
they were conducted. They were then promptly translated into
English (Luria 1976). Though originally designed as a contribution to Marxist psychology, they also directed attention toward cultural conclusions which (had they been generally
known) would have accelerated the investigation of historical
oralism as identifying a distinct mode of consciousness with its
own rules.

Luria's Russian "collision" had been an experience drawn out
of a contrast between essentially nonliterate individuals and
literates who were using the Cyrillic alphabet (that is, a variant

of the Greek). The split between nonliterates and literates was dramatic. More than a generation before Luria, a Frenchman who had chosen to live in the Near East and who had close sympathetic ties to it subjected himself to a parallel though not identical experience (Jousse 1925). This time the contrast was not between literacy and nonliteracy but between his own achieved literacy and what one might style "craft-literacy" or literacy of a secondary type in the environment he encountered. He was living in a cultural setting where writing had been used for centuries—that is, North Semitic scripts, Arabic, Aramaic, Hebrew. According to those who insist that such scripts are alphabets, his environment should have long become literate in the full sense of his own French model. But it only achieved some approximation to that model. That is why it seems appropriate to consider him in succession to Luria although chronologically prior, for he employed himself with a more "advanced" and complex cultural situation. What in fact he experienced and recorded with sharp, sensitive perception was the pervasive survival of oral modes of managing language and of a corresponding oral "consciousness." The syntax of the language was activist and dynamic (to employ terms later applied by myself to Homer); the culture which expressed itself in this way he styled "verbomotor," in contradistinction to the static categorical language characteristic of achieved literacy. Oral composition and performance of oralized language (if the expression may be allowed) was common. In these performances he noted the coordination of rhythmic patterns with the physical motions of the body (as later described from a theoretic standpoint in Havelock 1978a, pp. 39–40).

What then was the role of the writing system that was simultaneously in use? Does the paradox point to the conclusion that the system was and is inadequate in that it could not supply a foundation for literacy on the French model (which used the Greek alphabet)? Did this point to a further conclusion that the Greek invention, when it displaced the script from which admittedly it had derived many letter shapes, gained literate properties denied to its predecessors?

Lawrence of Arabia, operating in a similar cultural milieu during World War I, living in the desert among nomads, observed that the chanting of formulaic verse with musical accompaniment was used functionally in a military context as a means of organizing troops for action (see Havelock 1963, pp. 139, 144).

If we jump ahead from Arabian nomads to Oxford philosophers in the 1950s and 1960s we can be tempted to see a connection in the awakened interest of analytic thinkers in spoken language. The tendency is perceptible in the later speculations of Wittgenstein. When J. L. Austin proposed (1961) that "performative" statements constitute a separate category, he was identifying what was later to be perceived as perhaps a fundamental characteristic of orally preserved communication, where it has served as a necessary instrument of memorization.

The scene transfers itself to Canada (Havelock 1982b). Harold Innis, a distinguished Toronto economist, would seem an unlikely candidate to embroil himself in the oral-literate question, unlikely to commit his intellectual energies, in the last few years of a life tragically shortened, to historical exploration of the role of orality in previous human cultures. Yet the connection with his own professional interests was there, arising out of a growing conviction that modes of communication, the "bias of communication" as he called it, played a role at least equal to that of economic activity in the formation and direction of human society (Innis 1951).

Was there even here an effect of cultural collision, created in the folkways of Innis's native country, to which in its pioneer character and its anticolonial achievement he was passionately attached? In the communities of small-town people among whom he grew up he saw a personal identity and validity in language and communication which he thought was being eroded by the technology of the popular press and of newsprint, of instant news which fostered instant shallow thinking—all these the result of popular literacy. Starting from a tension within his own present, he extrapolated it into history going backward to the Greeks, to Mesopotamia, to Egypt, to Assyria, wherever he could find grist for his mill.

As a professional Innis had intensively studied the Canadian pulp and paper industry. As a patriot he thought he saw his native country's forests being destroyed to make a moment's shallow reading on a New York subway. In effect, he was evoking the specter of a print culture of the roller presses and warning against its corruption (Havelock 1982b, pp. 32–34). In this respect, McLuhan became his pupil so far as he was willing to locate an engine of social change in the printing press. But McLuhan's printing press of movable types was not the roller press of Innis. When, in effect, he attacked the printed book and saluted a release from it afforded by modern technology and particularly electronic technology, he was standing Innis on his head.

6

Can a Text Speak?

Aside from the paradox by which language has to be used to understand language, that is, to understand itself, we face a comparable dilemma when we undertake to understand orality. For the chief source material provided for inspection is textual. How can a knowledge of orality be derived from its opposite? And even supposing texts can supply some sort of image of orality, how can that image be adequately verbalized in a textual description of it, which presumably employs a vocabulary and syntax proper to textualization, not orality?

The same problem of contamination by literate idiom lurks behind the reporting by anthropologists and ethnologists of the stories and songs of the "primitives" they studied in America, north and south, and in Polynesia. These inevitably suffer some manipulative interpretation which may (though not invariably) recast the native idiom in order to extract its "meaning" for the modern mind. The introduction of the tape recorder might seem to overcome this difficulty until two things are realized: (1) the literate scientist still seeks an interview or audition with an individual, which he sets up; (2) his respondent commonly seeks to oblige him by supplying, in oral improvisation, the kind of information he thinks, quite correctly, that the researcher expects or wants.

Again, some tribal communities that seem to furnish functioning examples of "primary orality" actually employ a language that has been compromised by the written tradition of adjacent cultures. The *Myth of the Bagre,* for example, as reported and transcribed by Goody (1972), carries in its design evident traces of Moslem tradition and theology.

There always remains an insurmountable barrier to the understanding of orality. The Brazilian Indians sporadically studied by Lévi-Strauss between 1935 and 1939, as well as the American Indian and Polynesian and African tribes who have figured in other reports, exemplify societies which either never charged themselves with the responsibility of maintaining a developed and complex culture or have ceased to do so. In the former case, they have remained content with simple social structures, which did not require the support of a developed orality with a complex vocabulary. In the latter, having come into contact with literate cultures which have either invaded or infiltrated them, they have surrendered control of their economy, military protection, and legal system to governments that are literate in their methods of management. The surviving orality of such societies, whether African, American, or Polynesian, ceases to be functional, that is, to carry the responsibilities of a memorized code of behavior. The great epics, the chanted choruses, the ritualized performances, slip into forgetfulness. By the time the literate investigator reaches them to record what they are saying, all that is left is residual entertainment, stories, songs, and anecdotes which are not saying anything very important (Tedlock 1977; Havelock 1978a, pp. 337–38). The language used is no longer a governing language. It can, however, with the help of literacy, be modeled into forms that are attractive and interesting and have an appeal both aesthetic and romantic.

It is, of course, true that in primary orality, functional content is cast in verbal forms designed to assist the memory by conferring pleasure: social and aesthetic purposes form a partnership. Once social responsibility starts to be transferred to a literate class, the balance is altered, in favor of the aesthetic. The resultant product has encouraged the conception of an "Oral Literature," visible in the title assigned by Ruth Finnegan to her pioneering collection of texts (1970). The formula is surely a contradiction in terms, "as though oral creations were variants of written productions" (Ong 1982, p. 8). Although Finnegan herself has become more cautious, she still defends the product as representing what is valuable in orality, the original forms being beyond recovery, "if such ever existed" (Finnegan 1982). Once one takes a functional view of these forms, one concludes they would have had to exist, and indeed a likeness of their existence emerges even if unintentionally in some of the impressions carried home by early explorers, as for example in Cook's *Voyages*.

Between 1932 and 1940 the two Chadwicks had compiled a magisterial treasury in two volumes, containing, in Ong's words, "traditional oral stories, proverbs, prayers, formulaic expressions" (1982, p. 11). Here surely was a text which might "speak." But the title chosen for this work, *The Growth of Literature*, itself indicated how compromised the content might be and how strong the literate bias of those who transcribed it.

There is a different kind of text, not collected from the historical past but existing in the literate present—at least to the end of the eighteenth century—which has carried some (not many) of the hallmarks of orality. Rhetorical composition ever since the Hellenistic Age served as a discipline for higher education. It has fostered oral discourse and argument as performed for listening audiences. Yet the model texts used for this oral purpose are still texts readable and read. They have not escaped the paradox. Can they yield secrets of what true orality might have been like? The answer, as it has been explored in this field par excellence in the works of Walter J. Ong (1958, 1967, 1971, 1977), remains ambiguous and doubtful. One dividing line that separates all rhetorical practice from primary orality is obvious: the language used is prose, never formally poetic. But it contains enough poetic infusion to establish a linkage with orality, and to supply some clues to the rules by which oral communication at the primary level is managed.

Yet texts have been made to speak, after a fashion. Indeed, they were first "published" by being read aloud. The audience who listened carried the word to others. Copies of texts were borrowed to form the basis of further readings. Even the private reader recited what he was reading to himself as he read. The practice is fully attested through the Middle Ages (Clanchy 1979, part 2, chapter 8, "Hearing and Seeing"). Did these habits affect the style of the texts that were being used in this way, preserving vestiges of orality in a form of composition ostensibly literate? The phenomenon did not fail to attract the attention of two scholars writing within a decade of each other (Balogh 1926; Crosby 1936). But how can a text as such supply its own criteria for the detection of orality?

There is a category of concealed oralism of a quite different order which became preservable and open to inspection in the Hebrew tongue with the formation of the canon of the Old Testament, at a date still debatable (Pfeiffer 1941, pp. 51–65, versus Leiman 1976, pp. 125–26). Here are texts that do indeed "speak," but imperfectly. Genuine echoes from a primary orality long forgotten have been retained intermittently in a text otherwise devoted to revising them, epitomizing them, and incorporating them in a theological framework devised by a written tradition. They have even survived the effects of transliteration from Phoenician to Hebrew and translation from Hebrew to Aramaic to Greek (the Septuagint) and Latin (the Vulgate), before being further translated into modern tongues. Robert Pfeiffer identified the "Song of Deborah" (Judges 5) as "the only important historical source contemporary with the events described, before the time of David" (Pfeiffer 1941, p. 235). In a separate chapter (pp. 271–81) he identified and grouped together "The Poems of the Pentateuch." The "Jehovah Document," the oldest written source used in the Pentateuch, starting with the call to Abraham (Genesis 12), is described as "both an epic and a drama; it is an epic in style and subject" (p. 162). Isolated from the surrounding text and translated as a separate work, this became *The Hebrew Iliad* (Pfeiffer 1957) supporting an analogy with Homer's poem.

Yet this original is still a "text": it is presented as "the earliest *written* literature of the Israelite civilisation" (Pfeiffer 1941, p. 72; my italics), and its author is also described as the "Father of History" (ibid., p. 161), anticipating Herodotus— this with special reference to the narration of the reigns of Saul, David, and Solomon. But one cannot have it both ways. Either we have a Homer—which could be orality—or we have a post-oral historian. In fact the material is presented in prose, not verse, and in this form it must be pronounced to be non-Homeric and non-oral. Behind the account of the Patriarchs lurks "a saga of a bygone age" (ibid., p. 149). The "Pen of Ahimaaz" (so identified as the author of David's "biography") "appears to be largely dependent on legendary sources (Pollard 1957, p. 42). In short, the original oral material has been lost. What we have has already been remodeled as it has been placed in script. Except for Deborah's song, a few surviving poems embedded in the text of the Pentateuch, and the moving lament for Saul and Jonathan embedded in David's "biography," the oldest portions of the Old Testament fail to provide a model for primary orality.

Oddly enough, a millennium later when the first three books of the New Testament were written down it may be otherwise. Aside from the miraculous materials, these latter compositions are built around three chief components: the narrative of the Passion, a body of Sayings, and a body of Parables. Higher criticism of the New Testament was originally guided by the assumption that the gospels as texts are themselves composites of texts combined to form the final product. Oralism, we may say, was not "factored in" as a formal part of the investigation. This has been remedied with the recent publication by Werner Kelber of *The Oral and the Written Gospel* (1983), which in summary seeks to distinguish between a textual act—namely the narrative of the Passion—and a stratum of oral composition preserved in the Sayings as they were originally pronounced in Aramaic before translation into Greek. Whatever criticisms may be leveled at the details of Kelber's inquiry, the substance of it forces us to confront the oral problem as it existed in a Palestinian society 800 years after Homer, in a social context of orality which may be described as "secondary" (to adapt Ong's descriptive term).

Biblical texts considered as sources for orality offer a paradox of their own. The piety which they served encouraged continual rewriting of originals to bring them into line with a growing body of ritual, rules, and theology. But at the point where canonization sets in and the materials are frozen the remnants of oralism which, perhaps accidentally, have survived previous redactions are now guaranteed permanent survival.

The printed Bible was one of the first fruits of the Gutenberg invention, and no printed book has ever achieved parity with it. As print, it alone remains immune to McLuhan's critique. So far as it has been "backward scanned" (to use Goody's term) in "revised" modern versions, these have tended to render the retained oral poetry more evident to the reader, not less, though this may not be altogether true of the Sayings.

But otherwise, the introduction of print has had an opposite effect. The term "book" is commonly used by scholars to describe the papyrus roll and the parchment codex, as well as the contents of a modern library. Both script and print are "texts," but in print we see historically a gradual alteration in style and content. To what extent must it be viewed as "revolutionary"? Commonly, the printed text had been accepted as exemplifying simply a superior, that is, more fluent method of transcription. That something new had arrived in print was noted forty years ago by Chaytor (1945), followed thirteen years later by Febvre and Martin (1958). McLuhan (1962) dramatized what he thought this new thing was—the introduction of "linear thinking." Eisenstein (1979) has followed him by exploring, in two magisterial volumes, the social-political effects of print but without giving much attention to "the subtler effects of print on consciousness" (Ong 1982, p. 118). Harold Innis on the other hand, analyzing the effects of the roller press, had perceived that the problem had both a social-political and an ideological dimension (Innis 1951; see also chapter 1, above). Was the text as printed and multiplied, in whatever form, being robbed of any residual ability to "speak"?

A sense of it as something imposed on speech, perhaps hostile to the spoken tongue, has inspired the recent work of those styled both "constructionists" and "deconstructionists." Jacques Derrida (1967) in effect poses the question: Can a (printed) text truly speak? and answers No! His work recalls some things already said in different contexts by Barthes, Lacan, and Foucault (see Ong 1982, p. 165; Hartman 1981). But what one observes above all is the compulsive return to Rousseau (see above, chapter 5) whom Derrida would both embrace and reject: Rousseau had failed to perceive the true source of the "catastrophe"—the reduction of language to text. An "interior" consciousness has been forced outward and virtually destroyed. Behind the linguistic argument one detects in Derrida the accents of Freud, which do not form part of our story.

Derrida performs the service of stressing the romanticism which inspired Rousseau and has lingered on in the Lévi-Strauss perception of a mythic structuralism as a fundamental representation of the realities of human experience. But has he, any more than his predecessor, stretched his vision to comprehend that "primary orality" which supplies the original key?

One comes finally to two texts in ancient Greek transmitted like the Pentateuch from pre-Christian antiquity, which may have managed to conserve the substance of orality to a unique degree.

"Others abide our question, thou art free." The familiar cliché is no less true for being familiar. But what was the real secret of this Homeric freedom? Do these two texts really"speak"? The eighteenth century perceived that Homer's poems were composed and recited without benefit of letters. The perception entered philology with the publication of Wolf's *Prolegomena ad Homerum* (1795) and was supported by some insights in later philology. But the question still had to be put: Was it not likely that unlettered composition, rather than being a pale reflection of literate composition, would have become an art in its own right requiring the employment of its own verbal style distinct from any style employed in writing? A different way of using language in fact.

A youthful American scholar at the University of California at Berkeley set himself this question and supplied the first reasoned answer. Milman Parry, examining the text of the *Iliad* and *Odyssey,* discovered tokens of a persistent echo sounded in the recurring formulaic epithets attached to proper names. This was surely a technique of composition which was carried out orally without benefit of writing. The substance of the discovery was offered in Parry's thesis presented for the M.A. degree. The thesis was accepted, but he was made to realize that there was unlikely to be any future for him in the Berkeley classics department. He lacked the worldly caution of an Einstein, who as a doctoral candidate at Zurich prudently refrained from offering as his thesis his first paper on relativity, substituting instead the results of a routine investigation. In the eyes of classical scholarship, Homer was a text, and a work of literature. Parry departed for Paris, and there the reworked and extended thesis appeared in its classic form, *L'Epithète Traditionelle dans Homère* (1928). The friendliness of Paris at this time will not surprise those who note the nationalities of many of the "oralist pioneers" (as I venture to style them)—Lévy-Bruhl, Lévi-Strauss, Marcel Jousse, Febvre and Martin, and others. In fact, the same undercurrent of possible sympathy for oralism was visible in French linguistics. It was the presence of Meillet at that time which influenced Parry's migration.

Harvard, traditionally tolerant, was willing to support an empirical test of the thesis by allowing Parry (now an assistant professor) to visit and record surviving oral poetry as practiced in rural areas of Yugoslavia. Undoubtedly, it was this enterprise, appealing as it did to a contemporary bias among classicists in favor of empirical as against speculative methods of investigation, which forced the intellectual world to come to terms with what has been recently labeled "hard Parryism"—a rather silly appellation reflecting the strength of that textualist bias which prefers to cling to Homer as "literature."

Here then was a "text" transmitted as such from antiquity which nevertheless, taken as a whole, could "speak" in a way which the Bible as a whole could not. Are there any others like it, *Beowulf* for example? (Lord 1960).

Parry's later articles and essays, collected and edited by his son, with an extensive introductory review and critique of the long history of the Homeric Problem (A. Parry 1971), indicate that given time he might have gone beyond the acoustic mechanics of oral verse-making to consider what might be an oral state of mind and an oral condition of culture. His pupil and assistant, Albert Lord, has remained content to supplement the Parry analysis of verbal formulas by noting the formulaic character of Homeric (and Yugoslav) content, tracing the control over the narrative exercised by typical themes and episodes (Lord 1960). The discussion is kept for the most part within the context of stylistics. The poems are still "literature" albeit with a style of their own, namely an oral style. The paradox preserves itself in the title given to the institute at Harvard which houses the Parry Collection of Balkan Songs: The Center for the Study of Oral Literature.

Nevertheless, Lord noted and stressed the fact that the oral capacity of a Balkan singer who takes to writing is quickly corrupted, and that polite modern adaptations or imitations of oral poetry, especially in Italian, are not the real thing. This lesson, drawn from contemporary conditions, was applied to antiquity by Kirk in *Songs of Homer* (1962) and subsequent publications. Kirk argued that the act of oral composition in Greek was at once compromised and corrupted when it began to use the resources of writing. This foreclosed any possibility of the retention of genuine oral quality in post-Homeric Greek "literature."

The *Iliad* and the *Odyssey* in his view, while wholly oral, are also "monumental," the work of a "monumental composer." Since the metaphor of monument implies a physical and visible object (a large book which can be read) rather than a recitation of sounds as light as the air that carries them, the paradox already noted, which haunts all investigations of orality, still eludes solution.

7

Speech Put in Storage

In the schools of thought so far reviewed, orality, as it has been indirectly noticed, has been of that kind transacted between individuals, or between an individual and his (temporary) audience. The same has been true of the view taken of a reader's relation to his text, though the printed text has been more easily perceived to exercise social effects. Language itself, the raw "material" behind the script and the book, is identified as a means of communication that is "interpersonal": the problems presented by its transfer to writing of any kind become psychological. Even the binary oppositions of structuralism, though asserted to be universal, are presented as they lie latent in the consciousness of the myth-maker.

Yet language by definition is a collectivist activity; its conventions have to be shared by whole groups or societies of varying size before any of its "meanings" become available to individuals within the society. It would seem to follow that, while speech obviously is spoken by persons who may think they are speaking as individuals, and addressing themselves to individual interests, its primary function is likely to be one that serves collectivist purposes. The fact has been recognized by oralists and others only by a sort of side-glance, when they link the content of oralism to a "tradition," conceived as some kind of repository for myth and legend, but without being very clear as to what "tradition" is, or how it works. Is it the product of a group consciousness, of the kind envisioned by Jung, or of specific historical memories as, for example, of the Mycenaeans? To discover a more stringent and disciplined conception of what "tradition," either oral or written, may really be, one turns to Ernst Mayr's *Animal Species and Evolution* (1963), the remaining one of the five "break-through" works first discussed in chapter 3 still to be considered. As a whole, its purpose is the exposition of biological evolution. But in a kind of supplement, Mayr turns to consider what may be loosely termed cultural evolution (he himself avoids this formula), the process by which our species takes charge of its own development in order to produce human society (ibid., chapter 20, "Man as a Biological Species"). The mechanism of the process, the way it works, can be presented in terms of a model borrowed from genetics. The genes are programmed to contain biological "information" (p. 636) which in practice is transmitted from two combined parents to the offspring, guaranteeing the continuity of specific identity. Men do not gather grapes from thorns, nor figs from thistles. This information, however, has been accumulated by a group, a species; it is a common pool which individuals share. Evolutionary mutation, to be effective, has to be shared mutation.

The term "information" embodies a metaphor borrowed from the idiom of human culture and applied backwards to the genetic process. Hence, although from one point of view cultural accumulation (the "open" program, p. 636) can be explained on the analogy of genetic accumulation, from another point of view genetic evolution is explained on the analogy of cultural evolution. For present purposes, the key element in Mayr's account is the role played by the accumulation of information and its storage for re-use in human language. The conception had already been put forward by others, notably Julian Huxley; like oralism itself, it was a conception whose time had come. The appearance of Mayr's final chapter in chronological proximity to the four other works of the "break-through" was a happy accident, unassisted by any perception of connection.

What one next realizes is that the terminologies of "information" and "storage"—and also "re-use" (Havelock 1984, pp. 109, 110, 186)—insensibly imply that what is stored and re-used is something material: its language must then somehow be material also. This can come about when it is written, when it becomes documented. The same presumption lies behind the words "code" and "codification" and "encoding" and "imprinting" used to describe the kind of information that a culture "follows" (i.e. uses and re-uses), as for example a "law code."

The overall presumption is that civilizations to be worth the name have to be based on writing of some sort, have to be in some degree literate ones. Probably a majority of specialists who have considered these matters still share this view, including classicists. It is certainly true of the layman. When some advanced cultures like those of the Incas of Peru are observed to be wholly nonliterate, the lesson that might be drawn, namely that a civilized society with its own art, architecture, and political institutions need not depend on writing for its existence, is quietly passed over.

Once the necessity to preserve cultural identity through linguistic storage, on the one hand, and the oral character of early cultures on the other, are brought into conjunction and viewed together, the question arises: How then, can orality store its information for re-use? How can it preserve its identity? Since it can support a culture without benefit of writing, what are the mechanisms that supply the material function that writing later supplies, namely the provision of linguistic information which can survive.

Preface to Plato, though the first work to consider this problem, was published only at the same time as Mayr's work, and was unable to use the help of the formula embodied in storage-for-reuse. It had, however, proposed a metaphor of its own which essentially conformed to it, namely the "oral encyclopedia" (Havelock 1963, p. 319). Once more, paradox shows its head. A metaphor drawn from documentation on a massive scale is applied to a nondocumented phenomenon.

The clues which had prompted the formation of this conception were drawn from the texts themselves, both of Homer and of his successor Hesiod (assisted by what later Greek authorities, including Plato, had said about Homer). Hesiod addressed himself to the functions, as he saw them, of the Muses, whose utterance embodied the language of his day that he regarded as important. In addition to celebrating the gods (suitably so in the *Theogony,* a poem devoted to drawing up a long table of divine ancestry), they also commemorate *"nomoi* and *ēthea* of all."* Both nouns are part of the vocabulary of an orally controlled society, and as used here are untranslatable by any single modern word, but paraphrasable as "custom-laws and folk-ways." The ēthea carry with them the epithet *kedna,* which has the combined and contradictory senses of "careful" and "carefully kept."

But who are the "all"? Are they mankind, or, as the succeeding hexameter suggests, gods? The two hexameters conjoined after the oral manner form a masterpiece of ambiguity. Since the "folk-ways" are both careful and cared for, they constitute what we would call the "tradition" which the human society nurtures and is nurtured by. But tradition is also ratified and solemnized by divine authority, whether or not that authority is guided by it (a difficulty noted by recent scholarship; see West 1966, p. 178).

This formula of social function, used to describe a poetry which we normally view as inspirational and recreational, and which indeed is celebrated as recreational by Hesiod, seems unexpected. It matches the terms of the "instruction" assigned to the Muses and given to the poet when he first introduces them: he is to celebrate "the (things) that shall be and were before," a formula enlarged when put into their own mouths ("the things that are and shall be and were before"), which suggests a present tradition extending into the past and expected to extend into the future: The idiom in which the three periods are described establishes their identity, not difference.

These hints supplied by Hesiod, when compared with the content of the Homeric texts, seemed to fit, in the sense that so much of the Homeric narrative involves situations, scenes, and performance which are ritualized, that is, are not only described formulaically, but also rendered as typical of what the society *always* did under such circumstances. Individual "characters," as we think of them, express their purposes in typical terms, in a language of sentiments shared by the society (Havelock 1963, pp. 67–86). If they carried initiative and eccentricity too far, this uniqueness became a violation of the shared ethos (Havelock 1978a, pp. 19–22). Much of the thematic content, the epic motifs, noted by Lord (1960) turn out to occur in contexts that are social-political: they continually recall and itemize the rules of order to be followed in such things as holding an assembly, making a collective decision, conducting a banquet, arming for battle, issuing challenges, organizing funerals, and even carrying out such technical procedures as navigation, ship-building, house-building, and the like. The list is inexhaustible, even though in our imagination the narrative itself, kindled by the bard's skill, takes precedence over it. Such was the evidence which led *Preface to Plato* to conclude that the intentions of the Homeric epic were bifocal. On the one hand they were recreational: the poetry was product of an art designed to entertain, this being the preferred criterion by which modernity has judged them, usually adding the qualification that the entertainment is somehow mysteriously elevated. On the other, the poetry must also be seen as functional, a method for preserving an "encyclopedia" of social habit and custom-law and convention which constituted the Greek cultural tradition of the time when the poems were composed. *Preface to Plato* had two successors (Havelock 1978a and 1982) which were able to support this analysis by reference to Mayr's explanation of cultural continuity. The language of Homer is storage language devised orally for the purpose of survival.

Devising a spoken language for this purpose for contemporary Greeks was one thing; devising a means for transmitting its record to us was something else—a task undertaken by the Greek alphabet. This same instrument has made possible the formation of those concepts of information, of code, of cultural storage, by which oralism itself is to be judged. Surely, of all systems of communication used by man, the Greek alphabet has proven to be historically unique in its efficiency and its distribution. *Preface to Plato* (p. 129, using Householder 1959) had thrown out a hint of its superior efficiency, but only a hint. The author had not yet read Gelb's *A Study of Writing* (1952). While this work had explored and analyzed the evolving behavior of all known systems of script from Egyptian and Sumerian to Greek, the attention it gave to the Phoenicians proved crucial. Their writing, immediately preceding the Greek, was the most advanced of its kind, and is still commonly (though incorrectly) referred to as an "alphabet." The two peoples were neighbors in Asia Minor, so the Greeks were able to borrow the names and shapes of characters as well as part of their "values." But there was a crucial difference. Gelb applied to the Phoenician system the term "unvocalised syllabary," on the face of it a contradiction in terms, since a "syllable" by definition would seem to contain vocalization.

The art (or science?) of writing in the Near East had through millennia slowly promoted the invention of signs that had phonetic values, as distinct from the visual ones symbolized in early Egyptian hieroglyphs. Progress in this direction had got as far as identifying the syllables of a spoken tongue and assigning "characters" to them. The number of syllables is tremendous, and the resultant sign system became difficult to memorize and cumbrous to use.

The Phoenicians, searching for economy, cut down the number by inventing a shorthand, which grouped syllables in "sets," each set having a common denominator—or sign—representing the initial "consonant" of the set (Gelb 1952, pp. 148–49, speaking of "West Semitic"): for example, the five members of the set "ka ke ki ko ku" would all be represented by the sign *k*. The sign signalized the consonantal set, but not the isolated consonant *k*. The reader, therefore, who used the system had to decide for himself which vocalic to choose out of the five (or whatever number and variety of vocalics a particular language might use). Drastic economy (you would easily memorize the names of such an "alphabet") was purchased at the price of drastic ambiguity.

It is easy to see why pre-Greek systems never got further than the syllable. This "piece" of linguistic sound is actually pronounceable and so empirically perceptible. The consonants by strict definition are by themselves "dumb," "mute," "unpronounceable" (*aphona, aphthonga*—Plato's terms, borrowed he says from previous sources). The Greek system got beyond empiricism, by abstracting the nonpronounceable, nonperceptible elements contained in the syllables. We now style these elements "con-sonants" (*sum-phona,* the more accurate Greek term, replacing *aphona,* because they are "sounded in company with"). Their creation separated out an unpronounceable component of linguistic sound and gave it a visual identity. The Greeks did not "add vowels" (a common misconception: vowel signs had already shown up as in Mesopotamian Cuneiform and Linear B) but invented the (pure) consonant. In so doing they for the first time supplied our species with a visual representation of linguistic noise that was both economical and exhaustive: a table of atomic elements which by grouping themselves in an inexhaustible variety of combinations can with reasonable accuracy represent any actual linguistic noise. The invention also supplied the first and last instrument perfectly constructed to reproduce the range of previous orality.

Such was the argument, derived from Gelb's analysis, finally put forward (Havelock 1976, rpt. 1982a). The complete rediscovery of orality and oralism may turn out to be inextricably bound up with the "re-discovery" of the role of the Greek alphabet. But before that role can be fully understood, one obstacle remains, in the persistent reluctance by learned and layman alike to recognize the true distinction between the Phoenician and Greek writing systems. Reluctance was greatly reinforced when, hard on the heels of Gelb, David Diringer published *The Alphabet: A Key to the History of Mankind* (1953). This work in two volumes has won a wide readership. It committed itself to the view that the North Semitic systems of writing, which include the Phoenician (the exact filiation is hard to pin down on the available evidence), were indeed "alphabets" in the true sense of the word. The Greek system was merely an "adaptation" or an "improvement," not a technological breakthrough.

If the breakthrough thesis is accepted, it provides an explanation for the ambiguous kind of oralism which Marcel Jousse (see chapter 5, above) among others perceived as surviving to this day in the Middle East. We say "ambiguous" insofar as it exists in societies otherwise describable as literate, since they use script, and now print. If, however, the writing systems (Arabic, Sanskrit), derived as they are from pre-Greek Semitic systems, retain a traditional residue of ambiguity which requires expertise to interpret, the surviving oralism of the major part of the population becomes explicable.

Our review of the modern discovery of orality dating from the eighteenth century of our era brings us back to the Greeks. If any adequate visual representation of the way primary orality worked is possible it is to be found in the script they invented. Here in Greek are texts that truly "speak." What they first speak is likely to be a language shaped acoustically for storage, a language of preserved communication, a body of "useful" oral information. Equally, through this same alphabetic instrument, there was discovered a new means of storage infinitely more efficient than the oral kind which it had put into the record. The use of vision directed to the recall of what had been spoken (Homer) was replaced by its use to invent a textual discourse (Thucydides, Plato) which seemed to make orality obsolete. Here was a paradox indeed of dialectical process, of transformational change. The singing Muse translates herself into a writer: she who had required men to listen now invites them to read. There is justice in assigning her both roles. Was not the alphabet invented under her aegis, when her song was still supreme? Are we to deny her the credit for its invention and for the *ability to use it herself?*

8

The General Theory of Primary Orality

The language we speak as we go about our daily business is such a universal feature of our lives that we commonly do not think about it. If we do, our first idea of it focuses on the words we exchange with each other as we talk. We can extend our view to include a verbal exchange between one individual and a group, an audience, and then go on still further to think of it as something spoken silently, by a writer who writes down what he is saying so that another person can read what he says instead of just hearing it. Extended still further, it can become an electronic medium that speaks to me as I watch television or listen to radio. It is still the voice of an individual at any one moment (unless, of course, a choir is singing), magnified and speaking to me, another individual.

Employed in these ways, language is a phenomenon which operates as a means of interpersonal communication. Even at the electronic level, it is still a "talk show." From the beginnings of the human race, interpersonal communication was an occurrence between members of a family in the same dwelling, or as two or more people met each other in some public area— or, as society evolved, in town meetings or in a committee or in parliament or whatever. Its fairly recent technological extension across barriers of distance is now rightly viewed as a revolution in our lives and has given rise to a whole body of theorizing centered on the concept of communication, with its own research centers. There is even a "communications industry."

The genius of this unrehearsed conversational language lies in its expressiveness; its capacity to voice immediate sensations and impressions and feelings as between individuals, and also social modes and fashions and ideas as they are felt in the community. It is astonishingly flexible and mobile, and it always has been. That is what talk is. This is the kind of language that oralists commonly think about when they theorize about orality. It is the kind of language that textualists commonly think about when they oppose it to textuality. What, after all, is orality all about, if not a performance of a person's mouth, addressing another person's ear and hearing with his own personal ear the spontaneous personal reply? Here, surely, is the essence of communication, a process of spontaneous exchange, varied, flexible, expressive, and momentary.

A general theory of orality cannot and should not deal with this kind of language except incidentally. The clue to why this is so is contained in the word momentary. Oralist theory has to come to terms with communication, not as it is spontaneous and impermanent, but as it is preserved in lasting form. We become familiar with this form as it exists in our textbooks, our laws, our religious scriptures, our technologies, our history, philosophy, literature. We are brought into contact with some of it during our schooling. We may forget the details as we go about our adult business, but it is there at the back of our minds, a body of instruction taken for granted, the foundation of our behavior as human beings or, in a given case, as Americans, or other national human beings. This body of instruction changes, is added to, subtracted from, but slowly. Its fundamentals are permanent or seem so. They remain so because they are written down and documented in a language which is not spontaneous or mobile but rendered fixed, permanent, immobile, by the mere fact of its existence in script and, since Gutenberg, in print.

Of course, it can intrude into our daily talk, and often does. Any discussion of a serious topic is bound to use its terms, its vocabulary, its ideas. It slips so easily into our casual converse that when we cease to be casual, we normally do not think of the difference, but the difference is there—two idioms woven into one, but of separate genius, the one designed for immediate communication, the other for serious preserved communication.

Orality, by definition, deals with societies which do not use any form of phonetic writing. The Egyptian society in which the earliest types of hieroglyphic occur could scarcely use them for written communication, in any meaningful sense of the term, and the same is true of any society, tribal or civic, Polynesian or American, where archaeology can demonstrate the use of pictographs but nothing more than that. The common use of the term "writing" by specialists as applied to any and every form of symbolization without distinction has helped to blur the boundaries between primary orality, a distinct and separate condition of society, and its successors, the proto-literate, the craft-literate, the semi-literate, and the fully literate societies.

The accent is on the word "primary," which insists on a condition of communication that it is very difficult for the literate mind to describe or conceptualize because all our terminologies and the metaphors involved are drawn from an experience which is literate and which we take for granted. Literate habits and assumptions and language are the warp and woof of modern existence. One way of realizing the difference is to recognize that in primary orality, relationships between human beings are governed exclusively by acoustics (supplemented by visual perception of bodily behavior). The psychology of such relationships is also acoustic. The relation between an individual and his society is acoustic, between himself and his tradition, his law, his government. To be sure, primary communication begins visually with the smile, the frown, the gesture. But these do not get us very far. Recognition, response, thought itself, occur when we hear linguistic sounds and melodies and ourselves respond to them, as we utter a variant set of sounds to amend or amplify or negate what we have heard.

A communication system of this sort is an echo system, light as air and as fleeting. Yet we are given to describing its character and effects as though they were some kind of material existing in some kind of space. They become "patterns" and "codes" and "themes" and "monumental compositions." They have "content" and "substance." Their behavior becomes, linguistically speaking, a matter of "grammar," a term which by its very derivation betrays the source of its invention in the behavior of words as written, not spoken. Its rules are said to be "imprinted" on our brains. If preserved, it becomes "information," which is "packaged" and "stored" in the warehouse of the mind.

These metaphors and dozens like them are those of a literate culture which has long been used to looking at language as written, at that point where it ceases to be an echo and becomes an artifact. Metaphors are a necessary means of interpretive communication, but their constant use, in this case, illustrates the peculiar difficulty of thinking about primary orality and describing it. We lack a model for it in our own consciousness. Somehow, in using our language to describe oral language, we have got to construct, inside our own minds, the conditions of a controlled experiment in the manner of a chemist or biologist who strives to exclude any impurities, any unwanted bodies, which could compromise the process he is trying to isolate. But in this case, it can be done only in the mind, by recognizing the metaphors drawn from what is seen and touchable for what they are, using them only when we have to and vigorously correcting their effects.

The temptation to use them is reinforced by archaeology, which reconstructs cultures of the past by an inspection of visible ruins and the fossilized remains of organisms including man himself. Orality, as a functioning condition of society, does not fossilize until it is written down, when it ceases to be what it originally was.

By definition, it is no longer "primary." This must be as true
of Homer as it is of the scraps of early poetry in the Old Testament. As for the later verse—that of the Psalms, for example—this is all heavily compromised by conditions of composition which employed writing, despite the lingering
influence of oral rules and oral intention.

Can primary orality then be the subject of an empirical investigation in any serious sense? One can draw some inferences
about it based on an *argumentum ex silentio.* A lost culture which
survives for our observation through extensive physical remains
may be shown to have employed no writing whatever. One can
then consider, for example, whether the surviving architecture
and road systems indicate by their complexity a correspond-
ingly complex political structure. One can then ask, given that
communication systems in such a society were oral: Of what
kind must they have been to sustain such a political system,
sufficient to supply the information and the directives upon
which daily administration would rely? There appears to be
one full-scale culture of this kind still available to suggest
possible answers, namely that of the Incas of Peru. The question, however, in their case has not yet been put, nor, indeed,
have the physical remains themselves been fully uncovered or
studied.

A general theory must draw on an effort of imaginative re-
construction which relies heavily on extrapolation from our
present literate condition. Withdraw the use of the document
from our lifestyle and ask, "How could we live without it?" It
is partly a technological, partly a psychological question.
There is one small piece of evidence we can supply from ourselves. Until we are five to seven years old we ourselves are
oralists, pure and simple, albeit children dealing orally with a
world controlled by literate adults. What sort of language do
we use, or better, what sort do we prefer and enjoy during this
period? Especially, what kind of organized language do we enjoy? Does our childhood throw out any hints of rules which
once governed whole societies of adults for many, many thou-

sands of years? Take, for instance, the oft-noted desire that children have for listening to the same story again and again—a fact which even cassette manufacturers have had to take into account in dealing with the market for their products. Does it shed any light on the rules of language by which a society of primary orality lived?

A general theory of orality must build upon a general theory of society. It requires communication to be understood as a social phenomenon, not a private transaction between individuals. Language of any kind acquires meaning for the individual only as that meaning is shared by a community, even though the individual speaker is not addressing the community. Much of the attention given by textualists to orality as the counterpart or adversary of text is colored by Sigmund Freud's preference for seeking explanations for behavior in the hidden language used by the internal structure of the personal psyche. It is doubtful whether this bias can shed much light on the fundamentals of oralism even though the concept of "internalization" now plays a large part in contemporary discussions.

Once more we catch a glimpse of the romantic vision of Rousseau contemplating the sincerity, simplicity, moral integrity, of communication carried on between untutored savages. That is no way to visualize a society of primary orality. The Freudian methodology seeking the riddles of our human condition by probing into the inner realms of our internalized experience is reductionist in its assumption that a whole consists simply of the sum of its parts, that a society is simply an aggregate of its individuals. A general theory of primary orality is required to be dialectical, to consider the whole as governing the nature of the parts.

Society, oral or literate, exists as it succeeds in combining individuals into a nexus, which is coherent. It is not here today and gone tomorrow. By definition it is not a transient phenomenon, as a human being is, though its longevity in historical time has varied. Longevity relies on the support of tradition.

This word, with the concept it expresses, is taken for granted by all scholars and specialists. It describes an accepted presence in history. "Tradition" can be used to cover almost anything. The more ready its use, the more excuse it seems to provide for not going any further.

Few, if any, ask the question, What sort of thing concretely is a "tradition"? What is it made of? What is its actual substance? How does it work? They will fall back on the further concept of myth and leave it at that—except for Lévi-Strauss who at least argued that all mythology of the genuine kind has a common bipolar structure. If we ask to have the origin of the structure explained, we are told that it is the way our minds have to work, as they rearrange our environment and seek to understand it; reductionism again takes over.

Tradition has specifics for any given society. An individual has to learn what these are, whatever they happen to be. He does not draw them from an instinctive sensibility of his own, supposedly in tune with a vaguely conceived general consciousness. These figments of German speculation are of no help. One method of learning is visual. It consists of watching performance in order to imitate it, and it is very effective in the transmission of trades and crafts. It also works in the construction of domestic and public architecture. Successive generations go on building in a style of their predecessors which they can look at.

The other method is linguistic: you do what you are told to do, in this case by a voice which is collective, a voice of the community. This requires a body of language "encoded" (as we say in literate terms) to carry the necessary instructions.

The instructions have to possess stability. They have to be repeated from generation to generation, and repetition must be guaranteed to be faithful or else the culture loses its coherence and so its historical character as a culture. The language of the instructions must be so framed as to possess this stability. In literate societies this is no problem, since the necessary language is documented in law, scripture, philosophy, history, literature. How can this be managed in a society of primary orality?

Once inscribed, the words in a document become fixed, and the order in which they appear is fixed. All the spontaneity, mobility, improvisation, the quick responsiveness of spoken speech vanishes. The original choice and order of words can be corrected, but only by more writing which replaces one version of permanence by another (as in a word processor). This fixed verbal disposition in a visible artifact is the necessary instrument for supporting the tradition of the society we live in, a literate society whose continuity and character is stated and restated in a thousand documented supporting materials.

This kind of language has an importance which casual talk never has. When a society relies on a system of communication which is wholly oral it will, like ours, still have to rely on a tradition expressed in fixed statements and transmissible as such. What kind of language can supply this need and still remain oral? The answer would seem to lie in ritualized utterance, a traditional language which somehow becomes formally repeatable like a ritual in which the words remain in a fixed order.

Such language has to be memorized. There is no other way of guaranteeing its survival. Ritualization becomes the means of memorization. The memories are personal, belonging to every man, woman, and child in the community, yet their content, the language preserved, is communal, something shared by the community as expressing its tradition and its historical identity.

Educational theorists have often treated memorization as a dirty word, as though all it meant was repetition by rote of material lacking significance. No greater historical mistake could be made. Our knowledge of ourselves is badly served by such denigration. Not creativity, whatever that may mean, but recall and recollection pose the key to our civilized existence.

Literacy has supplied us with an artificial memory in the preserved document. We originally had to fashion our memory for ourselves out of the spoken tongue.

As written, spoken language becomes frozen in a fixed vocabulary and order. How, then, if communication is to be restricted to spoken speech, can spoken speech—that part of it to be preserved in order to become tradition—be adequately frozen to guarantee stability of statement?

Successful retention in memory is built up by repetition. The children who prefer a retelling of the same story desire to be able to remember it, and so be able to retell it in whole or part and so relish it. The repetition is linked with a feeling of pleasure, a factor of primary importance in understanding the spell of oral poetry. But mere repetition of identical content will not get you very far. The range of oral knowledge thus supplied will be limited. What is required is a method of repeatable language (meaning acoustically identical sound patterns) which nevertheless is able to alter its content to express diverse meanings. The solution discovered by the brain of early man was to convert thought into rhythmic talk. This supplied what was automatically repeatable, the monotonous element in a recurring cadence created by correspondences in the purely acoustic values of the language as pronounced, regardless of meaning. Variable statements could then be woven into identical sound patterns to build up a special language system which was not only repeatable, but recallable for re-use, and which could tempt the memory to lead on from one particular statement to a second, and a different one, which nevertheless seemed familiar because of acoustic similarity.

Such was the birth of what we call poetry, a performance now relegated under literacy to the status of a pastime, but originally the functional instrument of storage of cultural information for re-use or, in more familiar language, the instrument for the establishment of a cultural tradition. Having perceived   its   original   functional   purpose,   we   should simultaneously recognize its recreational purpose as also original. It is arguable that in its various guises rhythm (rather than the "emptying and filling" of the Platonic formula) is the foundation of all biological pleasures—all the natural ones, sex included—and possibly of the so-called intellectual pleasures as well. However that may be, its linkage to music and dance and its involvement with the motor responses of the human body seem indisputable. Accordingly, oral societies have commonly assigned responsibility for preserved speech to a partnership between poetry, music, and dance.

Acoustic rhythm is a component of the reflexes of the central nervous system, a biological force of prime importance to orality. Very early, it induced a secondary effect, by encouraging a supplementary habit of semantic rhythm, or balancing of ideas (or better, balancing of "notions," since "idea" is a literate term). One perceives it in the construction of certain maxims through balance of oppositions (as also in the familiar Greek idiom "on the one hand . . . on the other") and again in the responsive balancing of narrative episodes that have a family likeness, forming the thematic "patterns" observed by scholars of Homeric epic. Such compositional "systems" (another literate term) extend the echo device to the ideological level.

The effect is notable in Hebrew verse:

> Semantic parallelism . . . is a prevalent feature of
> Biblical verse . . . if the poet says "hearken" in the first
> verse, he is likely to say something like "listen" or
> "heed" in the second verse . . . some lines of Biblical
> poetry approach a condition of equivalent statement
> . . . thus, "he preserves the powers of justice—and the
> way of his faithful ones he guards."

Robert Alter, the scholar from whom I cite this observation, correctly goes on to point out that "the dominant pattern is a heightening of specification of ideas, images, actions, themes . . . instead of listening to an imagined drumbeat of repetitions, we need constantly to look for something new happening . . ." (Alter 1985).

This something new must occur as a partial echo of something already said: It is a "difference contained within the same," the "same" being the metrical beat or the thematic resemblance. This is the cardinal rule of the information language which primary orality places in storage, a rule enforced by the requirements of oral memorization: "If something is broken in the first verse, it is smashed or shattered in the second." To this example, adduced by Alter, one adds the converse type of balanced echo based on opposition: "The grass withereth, the flower fadeth, but the Word of the Lord shall abide forever."

How exactly ideological echo arises out of acoustic echo is a puzzling matter. The question goes to the root of the nature of the human consciousness. One notes connection with the binary opposition of structuralist theory; but the general theory of orality requires that the first foundations of binary opposition be sought in acoustic laws of memorization before we come to ideology.

Thematic echo on a far larger scale is employed everywhere in the Homeric poems: to give one of the more obvious examples, all the conferences between Achilles and his mother recurring throughout the extent of twenty-four books have a family resemblance. Yet within the resemblances, something new also occurs. The echo connection between them assists the memory to pass on easily from the first example to the second and to the third. The sequence registers itself as a sequence.

Language of this kind becomes a sophisticated instrument overlaid upon the vernacular of an oral society or, to change the metaphor, an enclave of contrived speech existing within it, the vernacular. The responsibility for maintaining it is likely to fall into the hands of specialists. These become the "bards of the people" (Heraclitus) and also the musicians, seers, prophets, priests. They guard the formulaic language noted by Parry as the basis of oral poetry—a language also likely to become a somewhat archaic one (as in Homeric Greek) since it is built on the instinct to conserve rather than to create and must exclude the casual idiom and unpredictability of current talk.

This language, what it says and the way it says it, itself shapes the tradition that guides social behavior; in fact it becomes itself the tradition. The Greek terms *ethos* and *nomos* identify its content more adequately than any other formula. The overall social nexus, supported by this memorized language, is largely self-regulating. But there also has to be some means and method of everyday administration, dealing with ad hoc situations as they arise: a summons to war, a decision to migrate, a solemn ceremony to avert plague; in family cases the settlement of disputed inheritances, a blood feud, a payment of debt. At various times a king or council of elders or a general gathering (an *agora*) becomes an instrument for making such decisions and settlements. But how precisely does the decision acquire form? How does it become something, the actual terms of which are known and obeyed? The decision needs some shape, however general. In early Europe, after literacy, it took the form of a rescript, ordinance, decree, or just "the King's writ." The terms of the directive were available in writing, which could be read aloud to an illiterate populace by heralds or criers.

The equivalent in societies of primary orality could only be composed in formulaic verse, or at least formulaic diction, rhythmic if not metrical, a proverbial type of utterance composed for the governing authority by specialists. This piece of storage language, the directive itself, is then distributed, by being sung or chanted aloud by heralds or criers. The poetic idiom would guarantee its existence and influence by faithfulness of oral repetition. The "decrees" of authority, in short, were sayings, suitable for memorization. By the time laws came to be written down, the idiom was becoming obsolete, its function of oral conservation no longer needed, but echoes of the style persisted in written forms for a long time. Sometimes the authority itself commanded the technique. Both David the king and Achilles the prince were themselves singers. Indeed, to be a master of sayings proclaimed and also of deeds done could become a direct avenue to political power.

By what means can the general tradition be taught and commended to the population at large so that they can share it and live by it? A primary assistance for this purpose is already provided in the technique employed. Its rhythms are biologically pleasurable, especially when reinforced by musical chants, by melody, and by the body motions of dance. When performed as a chorus the dance also has the advantage of involving whole groups in shared recitations and so shared memorization, a practice which continued to inform and guide the mores of Athens down to the age of Pericles. A high proportion of the youth of the Athenian governing classes received its secondary education in this way, as it was recruited for the choruses of tragedy and comedy.

The poets of orality were aware of their didactic function. The Muse, whose guidance they acknowledged, was their teacher and the teacher of their audiences. They were even more aware of the emotional impact of the poetry and music they employed. They took pride in the pleasure produced, which was the necessary accompaniment of the instruction.

Rhythm aside, their language utilized a second resource to assist memorization. Even at our literate level, the average adult would prefer to take a novel to bed with him rather than a treatise, because a novel relates a story, not a series of factual statements. The narrative format invites attention because narrative is for most people the most pleasurable form that language, spoken or written, takes. Its content is not ideology but action, and those situations which action creates. Action in turn requires agents who are doing something or saying something about what they are doing, or having something done to them. A language of action rather than reflection appears to be a prerequisite for oral memorization. The experiments and conclusions of Luria in Russia (see chapter 5, above) have only reinforced a lesson which the character of oral "literature" so called would have taught independently.

We tend to think of the oral storyteller as concerned with his overall "subject" (a literate term) for which he creates a narrative "structure" (again a literate term). The more fundamental fact of his linguistic operation is that all subjects of statements have to be narrativised, that is, they must be names of agents who do things, whether actual persons or other forces which are personified. The predicates to which they attach themselves must be predicates of action or of situation present in action, never of essence or existence. The formula "Honesty is the best policy" is a creature of literate speech, of documented speech. In orally preserved speech, this becomes "An honest man always prospers." More likely still, instead of being isolated in a maxim, the man's performance is incorporated in a story where he performs honestly (or fails to perform honestly).

The same narrative requirement has been observed at work in Hebrew verse. "There is dynamic movement within the line. . . . Causation is allied with temporal sequence . . . the same narrative impulse . . . often reappears . . . within the line" (Alter 1985).

One law of narrative syntax in oral poetry, noted by specialists, takes the form of parataxis: the language is additive, as image is connected to image by "and" rather than subordinated in some thoughtful relationship. But the parataxis habit is only the tip of the iceberg or (a better metaphor) the set of clothing which contains the living body of the language. This living body is a flow of sound, symbolizing a river of actions, a continual dynamism, expressed in a behavioral syntax, or (if the language of modernistic philosophy is preferred) a "performative" syntax. Recognition of it is essential to the formation of a true general theory of primary orality, one which also prepares us to confront a profound transformation that has since occurred in the nonperformative language we often use today.

In primary orality, the oral specialist, whether bard, priest, prophet, or seer, continually clothes his memorizable instruction in designs that are contrived to please; so that the instruction itself is fastened on the social memory by indirection, as it is translated into active examples. It should be noted that the examples which tend to predominate are in fact those in which the instruction fails to be carried out: the action that supervenes becomes "heroic" or "tragic" (or in the Hebrew case "sinful") but no less effective as a warning as it preserves and conserves the underlying "lesson."

Tradition in short is taught by action, not by idea or principle. For its teaching, oral societies have to provide suitable performance context attended by audiences who will be invited or invite themselves to share in what is on the one hand a language of specialists, yet on the other a language in which all to varying degree participate. The natural proclivities of human beings to enjoy themselves—and here again the pleasure principle is brought into action to assist the social need—give rise to common festivals and common feelings, feelings shared by all oral societies and central to their successful functioning, as they provide the necessary instructional situations. The festival became the occasion of epic recital and choric song and dance. The ritual feast can take the form of the symposium, a smaller collective association, a suitable vehicle for shorter verse and personal performance. On such occasions the verse of an oral society discovers its means of "publication," an accurate term for the process, though we think of it today only in literate terms, as the printing press and publishing house supplant the oral situations of the past by supplying a documented circulation among readers. The reader participates silently in the "performance" of the writer, whose performance is also silent. The oral audience participated not merely by listening passively and memorizing but by active participation in the language used. They clapped and danced and sang collectively, in response to the chanting of the singer.

9

The Special Theory of Greek Orality

In the history of the Greek written word, the earliest Greek text composed throughout as a text may be that of Hesiod, and this despite the fact that his language is basically Homeric, retaining all the formulaic character of orally preserved verse. It is all the more remarkable that in his verse he seems able to retain a vivid awareness of the orality that preceded the writing of his text, and even to recognize what its basic functions were, namely the preservation of tradition in the living memory. He does this in describing the persons and functions of the Muses for whom he composes his introductory hymn. To begin with, they are the offspring of a union between Zeus and Mnemosune, usually translated as "memory," as though the word were equivalent to Mneme (the other Greek word for memory). The fuller form signifies the exercise of memory as an activity, that is, "remembrance" or recall.

Parental inheritance, when commemorated genealogically in oral verse, was used to give a person (often a warrior) his own identity, indicating his social status and role in the community. The Muses, through their assigned parentage, are to be perceived as the guardians of the social memory, and since their behavior as described is wholly oral, without any thought of writing, it is a memory as preserved in spoken speech—that is, the storage speech required. The reason for their existence is not inspirational, as it later became, but functional. Appropriately what they utter is summarized as "the (things) of the present and the before" (*ta eonta, ta proeonta*), and also of "the to become" (*ta essomena*) which in its context with the other two participles refers not to novelty to be prophesied but a tradition which will continue and remain predictable (see above, chapter 7).

It is of some interest and relevance that this memory function commemorated by the early poet, but only symbolically and indirectly, achieved more explicit recognition later, after the passage of a century or more, at a time when the extended use of the alphabet had produced a rival means of remembrance in competition with the oral. One of the Promethean gifts to mankind is described as "compositions of *grammata*, Muse-mother, worker memory of all [things]." The *grammata* are "inscriptions"; that is, written letters. In these, the storage memory is now preserved. It has been transferred to their guardianship from the custody of oral language and has become overtly recognizable as a "memory" precisely because the letters as artifacts have objectified the memory by making it visible. But the fact that this is a transfer which still retains maternal orality, and not a completely new creation, is recognized in the phrase "Muse-mother," probably a recollection of Hesiod's genealogy. The term "worker," again, slight as it may be, recognizes for the first time that this language, whether oral or written, is something put to work; its role is functional, not inspirational uplift. The products of the alphabet (which included the Aeschylean play in which these words were written) are something more than just "literature" in our sense of the word.

By the beginning of the fourth century, literate intellectuals began to attend to the act of memorization itself, considered as a necessary technique to be learned. The need would only occur to them as the result of delayed recognition of an exercise that was slowly but surely becoming obsolete in their own day, but which in the oral centuries, sustained by a social pressure which was taken for granted, had itself been taken for granted, without achieving conscious recognition.

To return to Hesiod: the memory language of his Muses is, of course, rhythmic and in his terms is uttered in epic hexameters. The metaphors applied to their speech dwell on its liquidity; it flows, it gushes, in a steady stream. It is also a performance addressed to an audience—the gods in this particular case—on a variety of occasions, as in religious ritual (the hymn, which is what Hesiod is himself composing at the moment) or in a civic chorus (the dance) or as an epic recital, or as a song. The performances are musical, they have their accompanying instruments. The occasions are festive; you had a good time in feast or celebration or procession when the Muses spoke. These combined conditions are symbolically memorialized in the names that the nine are given: Cleio (Celebrator), Euterpe (Delighter), Thaleia (Luxuriator), Melpomene (Song Player), Terpsichore (Dance-Delighter), Erato (Enrapturer), Polyhymnia (Hymnal Player), Urania (Heaven Dweller), Calliope (Fair-Speaker).

The poet is commemorating, however indirectly, a system of social communication in a culture of primary orality in which such communication is shaped and performed to preserve the cultural tradition. It is a Greek situation. The inhabitants of Tahiti, at the time when Captain Cook visited them, would have understood at once what Hesiod was talking about though they would themselves have lacked the ability to frame such an account (Havelock 1978a, pp. 20–22, 31–32). How Hesiod himself could attain such a remarkable sophistication in this matter will require consideration (chapter 10). Though he either writes or has his composition written for him, he speaks of the oral situation as though it were contemporary. The date of his own composition is in dispute. Accepting the fact that the Greek classical culture began in total nonliteracy, how long precisely had this condition lasted? On this answer will depend a judgment as to just what the achievements of

Greek orality amounted to. Were they more formidable and long-lasting than is usually perceived? Does a special theory of Greek orality demand that we recognize its creative power in molding the high classical Greek culture which we now identify with Greek written literature?

If we place the nonliterate and the literate conditions in simple opposition to each other, one replacing the other, we vastly oversimplify. But at least the first problem to settle, if we can, is the date of the alphabetic invention, that superior technology of the written word, which first isolated the consonantal nonsounds and assigned them specific visible symbols (see above, chapter 7). It clearly precedes Hesiod's time as he could not otherwise have used it, and fairly copiously at that; but by how much?

Hesiod's, as I have said, may be the earliest text actually composed with the help of alphabetic writing. It is not likely to have been the first *piece* of such writing, however. The earliest surviving specimens of the classical Greek tongue so far known occur in five artifacts—a pot, sherds of two other pots, a fragment of (probably) a clay plaque, and a bronze statuette (Jeffery 1961, pp. 68, 90, 110, 235; Cook 1971, p. 175; Morris 1984, p. 34). The letters are incised, scratched, or painted; the dates of manufacture and of inscription need not necessarily coincide. The second can be later than the first, except in the instance of the plaque. This distinction is crucial in the case of one object—supposedly the earliest—the famous "Dipylon Vase," the manufacture of which has been set variously between 740 and 690 B.C. The earlier date or something near it has proved to be more acceptable. The vase is usually hailed as providing the earliest example of Greek writing. The other four objects position themselves around the date 700 B.C. plus or minus, and as a group they suggest a date of about 700 or less for the invention, in which case the Dipylon Vase was in use as a pot for some time before someone scratched the Greek letters on it—a reasonable assumption (Havelock 1982,

p. 15, quoting personal conversation with Jean Davison). To quote a careful authority (West 1966, p. 41), "there is only one known specimen of Greek alphabetic writing that need be dated earlier than 700." Even this need disappears once the object's manufacture and its use as a surface to carry letters are distinguished and treated separately.

In scholarly discussions of the date, the distinction has not been taken seriously. Considering the meticulousness which is the usual hallmark of classical learning, the omission seems remarkable. But it has the advantage of allowing the scholar to posit a date for the alphabet "in the eighth century" or "by the middle of the eighth century" rather than "the beginning of the seventh century." The reasons one suspects for this preference are ideological. It has two advantages: (1) it confines the nonliterate history of the Greeks as narrowly as possible, since nonliteracy, on modern analogy, is deemed unworthy of the honor of creating Greek civilization; (2) in particular, it allows the Homeric poems to be "written down" in the eighth century rather than later, which is felt to be more appropriate to their traditional content and their Mycenaean heritage.

One answer to the problem of dating the alphabet's invention which has been used and is commonly repeated can be illustrated from a notice published in the *New York Times Book Review* for October 6, 1985: "The Greeks themselves dated their history from 776 B.C., supposedly the date of the first Olympic games. It was about this time that the Greek alphabet was derived from that of the Phoenicians . . ." (MacQuarrie 1985). The text (of Eusebius) we actually possess which supplies this supposed information was composed in the third or even the fourth century of our era, well over a thousand years after the original event it purports to report. It has been argued that the source may have been a compilation of chronological lists drawn up by a Greek sophist at the beginning of the fourth century B.C. There is no evidence whatever that the Greeks of the classical age "dated their history" with this formula. More to the point, it has been observed that as late as the sixth century B.C. an inscription reveals the existence of civic functionaries named *Mnemones* (Jeffery 1961, p. 20), that is, "Remembrancers" (the Old English term) or memorizers (Havelock 1963, p. 52). Such a function presumes a service performed for a nonliterate society responding to a felt need to preserve orally not only rulings and precedents but some chronology of the past. This purpose is served by memorizing a fixed sequence of names with some associated events, often with a count of years added. The practice is illustrated in the genealogical lists of the Book of Genesis. Preservation and transmission would be effective and reliable only if entrusted to professionals trained for this purpose or training themselves. If the Olympic lists available in the fourth century B.C. did really go back to the first quarter of the eighth, their source was oral transmission, not alphabetic notation.

To presume that any kind of Greek literacy, however restricted, existed before the date of the first inscriptions is to rely on the assumption that the alphabet was applied to the surface of parchment, papyrus, or possibly wood and (if this assumption is used to explain early Greek chronology) that this usage occurred at least fifty years and probably longer before the letters were applied to hard physical objects. This, at first, may seem reasonable, given the possible loss due to perishability of the materials as against marble or fired clay. The literate context of our own culture again supplies an analogy which, though misleading, is powerful. The pages of a document have served for centuries as a source of authority. The inscription on an object or building is treated as decorative and incidental. So may not documentation have preceded incision or paint on a hard surface?

In Greek antiquity, one has the impression that for as long as two centuries after the invention of the alphabet the reverse was true. The habit of relying on engraved inscription for purposes of public information in Athens seems to have lasted through the fifth century B.C., one striking example being the redrafting of the Athenian law code at the end of the century. This would, of course, not absolutely forbid the notion that parchment or papyrus documents were in circulation before the epigraphical use appeared. If they were, this might mean that the professional singers themselves invented the alphabet (Wade-Gery 1952).

A plausible explanation recently offered by Kevin Robb (1978) has called attention to the act of dedication as a fundamental practice of oral societies and as a possible occasion for the invention of writing. In primary orality dedication could be achieved only by a public oral ceremony at which the object was presented and an address given in a language that the listening audience was likely to remember at least for a time. The same was true of the presentation of gifts. But in a bilingual community (in Cyprus or Crete or Al Mina) the Greek inhabitants saw their Phoenician neighbors dedicating such objects with written marks. Envious of the advantage thus gained— the object thereafter could speak for itself—they tried to adapt the trick to their own oral dedications, and the new alphabetic system was the result.

A dedication, oral or written, in effect assigns ownership of an object to the recipient and often identifies the giver as well. The names and/or the identities of the persons actually connected with this object, present or future, had to be put on record. The early group of epigraphic examples are all of this kind and moreover written in meter; they simply put into alphabetic characters a personal practice of primary orality traditionally supplied as a marginal service by bards and "rhymsters" (or rhapsodists?).

Admitting, as some scholars reluctantly now do, that the invention may postdate 700 B.C., the common presumption still rules—again following modern analogy—that thereafter its use became automatic: "The new invention spread very rapidly and from an early date a high proportion of the Greek people were fully literate" (Andrewes 1971, p. 51). The fate of orality when it comes in contact with literacy in modern times would seem to support this judgment. Contact between literate Europe and surviving nonliterate cultures occurred when European voyagers paid visits (Cook in Tahiti) or invaded and conquered (the Spanish in America) or when colonial powers colonized their "subjects" (Portugese, British, French, Germans in Africa). Only in the first case was primary orality left untouched and uncontaminated. The conquerers and colonizers did not sail away again but stayed and lived in close contact. Their superior alphabetic technology applied to the administration of the society which they governed swiftly supplanted the oral mechanisms of government with literate practice. The original oral performance with its poetry was stripped of functional purpose and relegated to the secondary role of entertainment, one which it always had but which now became its sole purpose. And so these vestiges have remained, romantic survivals available for the delectation of the tourist and the tape recorder of the anthropologist (see above, chapter 6). The very triviality of what survives strengthens the presumption of the classical scholar, if he notices the matter at all, that Greece had to be fully literate to produce a Homer and an Aeschylus.

The uniqueness of the Greek case needs to be understood. It is one which justifies the need for a special theory of Greek orality. "The Homeric epics considered as records of the orally preserved word . . . meet the following criteria of authenticity: 1) they have been framed in a society free from any literate contact or contamination, 2) the society was politically and socially autonomous both in its oral and literate periods and consequently possessed a firm consciousness of its own identity, 3) as far as responsibility for the preservation of this consciousness rested upon language, that language had originally to be a matter of oral record with no exceptions, 4) at the point where this language came to be transcribed the invention necessary for the purpose was supplied by the speakers of the language within the society itself, 5) the application of the invention to transcribe anything and everything that might be both spoken and preservable continued to be controlled by Greek speakers" (Havelock 1978a, p. 339).

No other instance of transition from orality to literacy can meet all these five requirements. The Tahiti visited by Cook met the first three, but only these. Recorded memories of oral practice in the Scottish Highlands fulfill requirements two and four. The surviving oral "literatures" in Africa fulfill requirements two and three. The effect in the Greek case, which is particularly to be noticed and emphasized, is the total social control retained by the Greeks themselves, both over their own oral life and over their alphabetic life. On the one hand, they suffered no pressure to adopt other writing systems as practiced by their neighbors. These were too inefficient to compete with their own invention, and no Greek statement that is extant is known to have been written in them. As late as the fifth century B.C. a diplomatic incident occurred between Greeks and non-Greeks (related by Thucydides) which illustrates the point (Havelock 1982, pp. 85–86). On the other hand, assuming that (1) the invention was a device of stonecutters and potters, who were the first people to possess the tools to apply it, and (2) they applied it upon the surface of artifacts new or old for purpose of dedications and the like, it would present no immediate threat to the time-honored linguistic technology of oral storage commanded by the professional bards. It offered no threat to the organized performance socially central to the culture. The alphabet was an interloper, lacking social standing and achieved use. The elite of the society were all reciters and performers. An anecdote in Plutarch describes how this was still true in the Athens of Themistocles (*Life of Cimon* 484a1). The organized teaching of letters in primary school is not likely to have occurred in Athens until the last third of the fifth century B.C. and is first attested by Plato in the early fourth (Havelock 1982, pp. 39–40).

All reasonable considerations point not to a ready acceptance of the alphabet but to a resistance to it which faded away at a rate to be determined by combining a great many indirect evidences. Reading, along with writing, treated as a human exercise which can be taken for granted, is not commemorated in Greek drama until the last third of the fifth century, in the *Hippolytus* of Euripides (see chapter 2, above). Primary orality departed only slowly from Greece, at a rate to be determined by the degree to which the written storage language replaced the oral storage language. Traces of inscribed "laws" (more correctly "rulings," that is *thesmoi*) survive in Crete from perhaps the late seventh century. The first coherent text (on a wall) is datable as late as 450 B.C. The so-called Constitution of Chios was perhaps inscribed a hundred years earlier. These epigraphical records, along with the Athenian "law code," as revised at the end of the fifth century, still retain, as previously noted, traces of formulations required when such rulings were a matter of oral memorization (Havelock 1982, pp. 205–06).

Under conditions of primary orality storage language is expressed in a complex of epic recitals, choric and ritual performances, dramatic enactments, and private songs "published" at symposia. It requires considerable social space. Its equivalent in letters could never be a matter of epigraphy. This afforded too restrictive a medium. Written storage had to find surfaces receptive of fairly copious and fluent transcription, which in antiquity meant parchment or papyrus.

There was also some restricted use of slate and wax tablets and even sand (recorded as in use as late as the first century of our era, if an incident narrated in St. John's gospel is to be trusted). But sand was obviously nearly as fleeting a medium as sound itself.

Inscribed on parchment or papyrus, the new writings contain the first texts of what we call great literature—but which the Greeks of the time naturally regarded as a continuation of that oral practice which was expected incidentally to provide didactic guidance for their culture. The "literature" as we think of it was also an instrument that taught *mousike*. The name "Hesiod" (see above, chapter 2) is commonly assumed to be that of the earliest identifiable author linked to a supposedly historical episode of uncertain date (West 1966, pp. 40–48; 1978, pp. 30–32). More plausibly, the first texts that can be firmly anchored to a definite personality and a determinate date (648 B.C.) are those ascribed to Archilochus of Paros (Havelock 1982, p. 103). Personal his verse may have been; nevertheless, the remains, scanty as they are, disclose a high proportion of exhortation, admonition, proverb, fable, and ritual celebration; in short, a continuing commemoration of the orally transmitted tradition of his day. His date does give support to the hypothesis that the alphabet did not become available till near the end of the first quarter of the seventh century. Even then its adaptation to copious transcription took time. The flow of texts—at least of those we either now have or can know something about—remained meager until the fifth century.

Of course, as in the case of the first inscriptions, it can be argued that much of very early literature has been lost. The so-called Epic Cycle surviving in later epitome is often cited in this connection, though the poems concerned may not be as early as is often supposed, and their record survives only from later antiquity.

It is relevant in this connection to observe that contrary to later and literate notions of their own past, the Greeks of the sixth and fifth centuries used the names Homer and Hesiod as though they designated two partners in a common enterprise (Xenophanes, Heraclitus, Herodotus, Alcidamas: this enterprise, according to their own notices, being instruction rather than entertainment). What they taught is condemned by the two philosophers but approved by Herodotus. Plato in the fourth century takes the same view of their joint function and, like his philosophical predecessors, disapproves of it. Heraclitus, moreover, in this same connection, treats Homer as a partner with Archilochus. The casual tone of the references made

by both pre-Socratic philosophers to Homer and Hesiod, and
to Archilochus, gives an impression—but only an impression—that they thought of themselves as not far removed in
time from the persons they were talking about. Heraclitus,
indeed, refers to Homer in one instance almost as though he
might still be alive. All of which provokes the suggestion that
neither Homer nor Hesiod as known in the late sixth century
could have been in public circulation much before that time.
By "circulation," of course, is meant publication through
acoustic performance, as Heraclitus makes clear.

The special theory of Greek orality therefore requires the
presumption of a long period of resistance to the use of the
alphabet after its invention, with the corresponding presump-
tions that (1) the language and thought forms of primary orality considered as a storage technology lasted on long after the
invention occurred (in fact, roughly speaking, and in atten-
uated form, to the death of Euripides); and (2) the character of
high classic Greek literature, its historical uniqueness, cannot
be understood apart from this fact. In the Greek case then we
face the paradox that, whereas the alphabet by its phonetic
efficiency was destined to replace orality by literacy, the first
historic task assigned to it was to render an account of orality
itself before it was replaced. Since the replacement was slow,
the invention continued to be used to inscribe an orality which
was slowly modifying itself in order to become a language of
literacy.

Precisely what these modifications were is a matter for the
next chapter. To our modern literate taste, if we are honest
with ourselves, the changes in idiom and vocabulary as they
occurred might be welcome. It is easier for us to read Plutarch
than Thucydides, Theocritus than Pindar. But before hasten-
ing to consider this development, it is necessary to understand
that the initial advantage offered by alphabetic efficiency was
to provide a script which could fluently and unambiguously
transcribe the full gamut of orally preserved speech. Anything,

any meaning, acoustically framed and spoken, any emotion or expression, could after being heard now be written down, as we say, "in full." Such complete visibility for language had not been developed in previous writing systems, and the consequent difficulty of interpretation had limited their use. They recorded simplified versions of the orality of their societies, the fulness of the oral originals being irretrievably lost.

That is why Greek orality requires its own special theory. Its transcription into the alphabet was historically a unique event. The Hebrew example furnished in the Old Testament is not a parallel case. The instrument of inscription was imperfect. It could not "hear" the full richness of the original oral tradition. The vocabulary as it is written shows a steady tendency to economize and simplify both thought and action. This adds ritual dignity to the record but at the cost of omitting the complexities of physical and psychological response, all the mobility and liveliness which are such a prominent feature of the record as transmitted in the Homeric script. The same limitation holds true for the remains of the Sumerian and Babylonian so-called "epics." The story of Gilgamesh illustrates the economy that has to be practiced (Havelock 1982, pp. 168–70). These versions were to be used and read and maybe intoned on ceremonious occasions by scribes but not recited expansively in festivals of the people.

Such scripts tend to ritualize their accounts of the human experience and so simplify it and then make this simplified version authoritative. Primary orality by contrast controls and guides its society flexibly and intuitively, and its alphabetized version in Greek continued this flexibility. The authorized versions offered in other scripts were more narrowly compulsive. They operated by imposing "the jot and tittle of the law." The original orality became compromised by doctrine and dogma.

The Greek story is free of this crippling factor. There was no single institutionalized priesthood and no attempt to form a canon out of what was being inscribed.

One can compare the account of creation in Genesis with the cosmic geography that occurs in Homer and Hesiod. The former is a standardized account, numerically simple, spaced arithmetically from one to seven. The latter records the variety, the unpredictability of the cosmos and its forces as they are personified in conflict or collision (Havelock 1981). The Genesis account is not of that kind which Hebrew singers would have originally sung for their people before the Phoenician script (or the Hebrew) took over the task of codification.

Since the Greek special theory requires us to recognize that the process of replacement must have been slow, we also have to perceive the survival power of orality in those masterpieces of epic, didactic, lyric, choric, and dramatic composition which we commonly regard as the written literature of high classic Greece. One begins with the obvious: Greek literature from its beginnings was composed in verse, not prose, and in Athens this continued roughly to the death of Euripides.

The first attested exceptions are all works written in Ionic, the authors in approximate chronological order being Pherecydes of Syros (if indeed his is to be "reckoned the first book in prose"; see Lesky 1966, p. 161), Hecataeus of Miletus, Anaxagoras of Clazomenae, Protagoras of Abdera, Herodotus of Halicarnassus, Ion of Chios, and Pherecydes of Athens. The list gives evidence that the writing of Greek prose originated overseas—evidence consistent with the conclusion universally admitted that the alphabetic invention did not occur on the mainland. It is a further reasonable inference that the cities of eastern Greece had a head start in its application and in the development of a schooling to teach it, of which these authors were the beneficiaries.

The content of the versified language—which, as versified, is storage language, regardless of the individual styles and purposes of individual writers—is uniformly mythic, meaning traditional. As Homer used a legendary Mycenae to give distance to the *ethos* and *nomos* being recommended to contemporary Greek societies, so also did his successors, composers of didactic, lyric, choric, and dramatic language. The dramas of Athens, under the guise of telling a twice told tale, addressed themselves to the *polis* of the day and its concerns. Pindar, composing choruses of address to his patrons, uses mythology to commend the contemporary virtues of martial and athletic valor, along with warnings against excess. Aeschylus celebrates the rule of law in the Athens of today as it takes over from the blood-feud of the Athens of yesterday projected backwards into Mycenae. Sophocles presents in the legendary Oedipus a Periclean statesman overcome by plague and his own self-confidence in his own policies. Euripides in his *Hippolytus* uses a legendary Athens of Theseus to denominate two competing standards of sexual conduct, as they were becoming perceptible in contemporary Athens.

Surviving orality also explains why Greek literature to Euripides is composed as a performance, and in the language of performance.

The audience controls the artist insofar as he still has to compose in such a way that they can not only memorize what they have heard but also echo it in daily speech. The language of the Greek classic theatre not only entertained its society, it supported it. Its language is eloquent testimony to the functional purposes to which it is put, a means of providing a shared communication—a communication not casual but significant historically, ethically, politically. It was a continual imitation (*mimesis*) of the ethos and nomos of the city (Vernant 1967, pp. 107–08; Havelock 1982, pp. 267–68) but carried out by indirection. In the theatre of Dionysus, the plays could not be put on until the same theatre had first been used for a civic procession and a public ceremony honoring the orphans of conflicts fought in the previous year.

Didactic function is focused most sharply, though not exclusively, in the Greek choruses, a continual rehearsal (*mimesis*) of the lawful side of Greek life (or of meditations upon it), sometimes only loosely connected with the plot. These constituted the core of the play, too often treated in modern literate adaptations as peripheral to it, but never so in classical Greece.

Athenian prisoners of war in Sicily, according to Plutarch's anecdote, gained their freedom from their captors by their ability to recite the choruses of Euripides—not the dialogue or the speeches. Here was the traditional language they found most easy to memorize, not because they had read it—the first reference to the silent reading of a play occurs at the very end of the century (Havelock 1982, p. 204)—but because they had heard it, and not just once. Repetitions of dramatic performances in the countryside were regular in Plato's day; he says so himself (*Republic* V.475d). A century earlier, one famous performance in Athens—the *Taking of Miletus*—proved so overwhelming that its reenactment was forbidden. The dramatic festivals preserved the means by which primary orality controlled the ethos of its society through a repeated elocution of stored information, guidance preserved in living memories. It is a tribute to its effectiveness and the spell it cast that construction of physical facilities suitable for such performance continued to be a feature of the Hellenistic age. The Greeks had to have their theatre.

Above all, the sense of primary orality survived in the behavior of the Greek tongue itself as it was being written down. Greek drama offers no propositions, beliefs, or programmed doctrines in the style of a Dante (still more of a Milton) but an expressive dynamism whether in word or thought. It is difficult to find an instance of a conceptual subject attached to a conceptual predicate by the copula "is" anywhere in the plays. The verb "to be," if it is used, still functions preferably in its oral dynamic dimension, signifying presence, power, situational status, and the like.

The absence of any linguistic framework for the statement of abstract principle confers on the high classic tongue a curious and enviable directness, an absence of hypocrisy. The particularism of orally remembered speech has the continual effect of calling a spade a spade rather than an implement designed for excavation. The speech will praise or blame but not in terms of moral approval and moral disapproval based on abstract and manufactured principles. A character in Greek drama does not theorize himself out of an unpleasant situation. He walks into it with motives that are specific and, if he has to, later accepts it when he recognizes what has actually happened.

Translation of the high classical language into a modern literate tongue, when the effect is compared with the original, at once brings out the dynamics of the oral tongue and what has happened in the transfer to a literate syntax. Oedipus opens the play that bears his name with a public address in which he describes the city's condition: "The town is heavy with a mingled burden of sounds and smells" (Grene 1954). In the English of this widely used modern version a subject, "town," is presented and given its predicate, the attribute "heavy" connected to it by the copula "is"; and the predicate is qualified further by the phrase "with mingled burden" which is added to it. The grammatical structure is atomistic, item is added to item using the connections supplied by the verb "to be" and the preposition "with." The whole effect is static. Meaning is accumulated piece by piece. The original Greek says: "The city altogether bulges with incense-burnings." The imagery is dynamic: the city turns itself into a pregnant woman or a packed container.

The speaker then continues (in the English version): "I did not think it fit that I should hear of this from messengers"; that is, he states a proposition which he had formed mentally, which requires an impersonal "it" as part of its idiom and requires to be explained by a subordinate clause introduced by "that." The Greek says, "What [things] [I] adjudicating not from messengers other [than you or myself] to hear." A language describing active mental effort has been replaced by an objective "think it fit that. . . ." The word "other" (in the Greek) contains a dynamic ambivalence: "I want to hear only from you: I want to hear by myself." Modern literate idiom enforces a choice: one or the other, but not both.

The English version then continues: "You are old and they are young," a propositional definition of two groups of people requiring the verb "to be" twice over. The original Greek expresses a simple call from one person to another to whom he applies verbs of dynamic process: "Oh aged sire, speechify. You have grown appropriate to pronounce in front of these here" (pointing). In this way Oedipus evokes the living presence and nature of the elder that he is confronting, in contrast to himself.

He then pronounces his last line, before the priest is allowed to speak his piece. It opens emphatically with the verb "to be"—not, however, the colourless copulative monosyllable of our tongue but a word of two full quantities sounded like a trumpet and placed at the beginning of the iambic line, proclaiming his existence, his presence, and his stature and status as their ruler. "Unpainable would I exist." In literate translation, this becomes "I would be very hard"; all the color has gone out of it.

Such examples could be multiplied a hundredfold. They demonstrate that classic orality is untranslatable. It is far easier to translate Plato. The propositional idiom with the copula which we continually fall into is precisely what Plato wished the Greek language to be converted to, and he spent his entire writing life trying to do this. When he turns against poetry it is precisely its dynamism, its fluidity, its concreteness, its particularity, that he deplores. He could not have reached the point of deploring it if he had not become literate himself.

Since Sophocles' day, much has happened to the speech of the mind and to the mind itself. While retaining the language of doing, of action or feeling in part, we have supplemented it, and partly replaced it, by statements of fact. The participles and the verbs and the adjectives that behave like gerunds have yielded to conceptual entities, abstractions, objects. Oral Greek did not know what an object of thought was. The Muse, as she learned to write, had to turn away from the living panorama of experience and its ceaseless flow, but as long as she remained Greek, she could not entirely forget it.

10

The Special Theory of Greek Literacy

How the human mind really works, how what we call "thoughts" are formed, is a mystery not easily penetrated. Philosophers of many persuasions would prefer to separate mind from our senses and treat it as an autonomous self-regulating "entity," to be understood and investigated as such. This involves the paradox that the mind would undertake to understand itself. Is this a logical impossibility, or a metaphysical absurdity? It seems to have been an objective proposed by Socrates of Athens as early as 430 B.C.

A special theory of Greek literacy involves the proposition that the way we use our senses and the way we think are connected, and that in the transition from Greek orality to Greek literacy the terms of this connection were altered, with the result that thought patterns were altered also, and have remained altered, as compared with the mentality of oralism, ever since.

One begins with the Darwinian maxim, that our human capabilities have been produced by the pressures of natural selection exercised over perhaps a million years. The major specific differentiation that has occurred lies in our capacity for linguistic communication, which in turn brings into existence that kind of society enjoyed specifically by man. With society comes culture in all its manifestations. Though many of these are material (art and architecture, for example) the act of communication which they indirectly express depends in turn upon the activity of linguistic communication. Human language is the foundation; the material achievement is the superstructure.

"Spoken or written" is a phrase which, when one thinks about it, calls up a problem in elementary psychology. The acoustic form of communication to which orality is confined employs ear and mouth, and only these two organs, and depends on them for its coherence. Written communication adds the vision of the eye. Is this a simple sum in addition or conversely a simple sum in substitution, one factor in the equation being simply replaced by another?

If the laws of evolution are taken seriously, neither can be wholly true. The acquisition of that means of communication which is specific to man was accomplished by "an increase of brain size during the mid-Pleistocene at an unprecedented rate. Average cranial capacity rose from a thousand to 1,400 cubic centimeters in less than one million years" (Mayr 1963, p. 634).

In parallel, selective pressures altered the shape and use of the face. Before man, the mouth in living organisms had developed as a means of mastication and as a weapon to grasp or kill the food required as well as defend it. Some secondary specialization occurred which allowed very elementary acoustic communication—the bark, the growl, the warble, and the like. The adaptations required for human language included "the low position of the larynx, the oval shape of the teeth row, the absence of diastemas between the teeth, the separation of the hyoid from the cartilage of the larynx, the general mobility of the tongue and the vaulting of the palate" (ibid., p. 635).

To be sure, human communication relies also on vision to the degree that bodily signals and responses are perceived by the eye. That could never of itself create human society, nor our essential humanity. It is a fact of our biological inheritance that these emerged through the use of our ears and mouths. To suppose that after a million years, vision employed on a physical artifact—a piece of writing—could suddenly replace the biologically programmed habit of responding to acoustic messages, that is, that reading could replace hearing, automatically and easily, without profound and artificial adjustments of the human organism, is to fly in the face of the evolutionary lesson.

As the change toward literacy has occurred, it has produced changes in the configuration of human society. These, particularly as they have arisen after the invention of print, have attracted notice from recent scholars and historians (see above, chapter 6). But the main shift began to occur with the invention of writing itself, and it came to a crisis point with the introduction of the Greek alphabet. An act of vision was offered in place of an act of hearing as the means of communication, and as the means of storing communication. The adjustment that it caused was in part social, but the major effect was felt in the mind and the way the mind thinks as it speaks.

The crisis became Greek, rather than Hebrew or Babylonian or Egyptian, because of the alphabet's superior efficiency. Fluency had always characterized orally formed communication. To achieve a complete transfer to a system of visual recognition required a comparable visual fluency. This the pre-Greek systems could not provide, and so they could not compete adequately with the oralism which they partially recorded but which continued to flourish as the habit of a majority. Even today this seems to hold true in societies that are not officially alphabetized (see above, chapter 6).

Granted that primary orality had subsisted as a biologically determined condition for an undetermined period of evolutionary time, and that its social effectiveness depended upon a tradition acoustically memorized, the dramatic and traumatic effect of substituting a written artifact for this purpose becomes obvious. Aside from adding the vision of the reader as a third sensory means, it wiped out, at least theoretically, the prime function of the acoustically trained memory, and therefore the pressure to have storage language in a memorizable form. As the memory function subsided, psychic energies hitherto channeled for this purpose were released for other purposes.

The initial effect of the invention had been to record orality itself on a scale never before attained. The special theory of Greek literacy describes a situation of unique complexity. The powers of "written orality" (if the paradox be allowed) were strong enough in Greece to enforce a partnership with the newly discoverable powers of the alphabet. What precisely these latter were is the subject of this chapter, but to isolate them as a "revolution" (as in Havelock 1982), while theoretically convenient, does injustice to the unique genius of classic Greek literature. The masterpieces we now read as texts are an interwoven texture of oral and written. Their composition was conducted in a dialectical process in which what we are used to think of as "literary value" achieved by the architectural eye crept into a style which had originally formed itself out of acoustic echoes.

The removal of pressure to memorize, registering slightly at first and very gradually increasing its force, had as its first effect some removal of the corresponding pressure to narrativize all preservable statement. This had freed the composer to choose subjects for a discourse which were not necessarily agents, that is, persons.

They could in time turn themselves into names of impersonals, of ideas or abstractions or "entities" (as we sometimes call them). Their prototypes had occurred in oralism, but only incidentally, never as the subject of the kind of extended language allotted to persons.

Hesiod affords an initial example of a process which was to gather momentum later, when he chose the term *dike* (usually translated "justice") as the formal subject of a "discourse." The term occurs incidentally and not infrequently in orally preserved speech (as in Homer) but never as the topic of a formal discussion. The narrative laws of oral memorization would discourage such a choice.

Having made his choice, Hesiod cannot conjure the required discourse out of thin air. We could easily manage it today, because we inherit two thousand years of literate habit. He, on the contrary, must resort to the oral word as already known—the only preserved word that is known. He must build his own semi-connected discourse out of disconnected bits and pieces contained in oral discourse, either some pieces in which the term *dike* happened for whatever reason to occur, or others in which incidents occurred that he felt were appropriate to connect with the word. His decision is compositional (rather than ideological), or perhaps we should say re-compositional.

If he must do this, he will be forced to continue to utilize the narrative forms which control what he is borrowing from. He still will not be able to tell us what justice is, but only what it does or suffers. He has taken one decisive step toward the formation of a new mentality by inventing the topic to take the place of the person. But he cannot take the second step of giving his topic a syntax of descriptive definition. It will still behave rather than be. So in seventy-three lines of hexameter we are treated to a panorama of dynamic situations in which justice singular or plural features as a subject performing or an object being performed on: a voice speaking, a runner in a race, a woman abused, a present you give someone, a thing you walk away from, a pronouncement of Zeus, a crooked weapon to inflict injury, a ward protected by guardians, a virgin goddess who sings her proclamations, a prisoner confined, a piece of property, a present given by Zeus to men, a cripple. The heterogeneity of the images may seem to be a symptom of confusion, but in fact it is the product of new invention, unavoidable at the first stage of a pioneering journey of language and of the mind (Havelock 1978a, chapters 11 and 12).

The psychological push needed to bring this about must

have been the use of vision as supplement to hearing. An architectural—not acoustic or at least only partially acoustic—rearrangement has been performed on language as previously used. The various "justices" which perform one after the other in Hesiod's account echo each other acoustically to some extent, but they are also all "look-alikes." The reading eye has been able to perceive them as located in an oralistic flow that has now been written down in the alphabet, which can be looked at, read, and "backward-scanned." Hesiod could have so composed only if he was able to "read" oral texts of Homer (and perhaps others), though not necessarily the complete Homer of today.

The first beginnings of the alphabetic revolution have occurred, in the creation of a *topic* as a subject of a "discourse" made possible by the conversion of acoustically preserved memorized speech into materially preserved visible artifacts that are capable of rearrangement. But the topic must continue to behave as a person or as something managed by persons. Partnership between oral and written, acoustic and visual, ear and eye, still remains intimate, with the eye as yet a junior partner. As the partnership develops and the ratio of control slowly alters, topicalization slowly increases its presence in classic Greek. The effect can be dramatized by a particularly famous illustration—the chorus on the genius of man, composed to form the first stasimon of Sophocles' *Antigone*. Here is a topic presented formally at the beginning (333). It is named *anthrōpos*, also styled later as *anēr* (348).

This general kind of "person" can crop up briefly in oralist language—Homer for example—by being included in a maxim: "As (is) the generation of leaves, such also of men. . . ." The maxim indeed comes nearer to the nature of an abstract statement than anything else in oralism. But its determinate characteristic is its brevity. The mental operation involved in thinking it up means breaking away briefly from the flow of the narrative panorama in order to fix it in some permanent posture, and the effort could last only a brief time, before relapsing into the familiar habit of memorizable narrative.

Here, however, in Sophocles' verse—and in highly memorizable cadences—is an extended topic. This creature is a phenomenon (333). His thirteen achievements, or hallmarks, are itemized not necessarily in logical order: first, navigation, followed by agriculture, bird watching, hunting, fishing, domestication of animals (the sustenance group); then language, thought, social instincts, architecture, medicine, law, the state (*polis*).

Clearly, in this example, echoes of an anthropological discourse have intruded into the play's text. They even include a reference to the achievement of technical skills (365–66). However, though a topic "man" is proposed and described, we are never told what it (or he) "is," only what this named "person" *anthropos* "does." A series of man's properties as a species is spelled out in short narratives of things we do. Even man's *noema* (thought) is "wind-swift." These are not definitions, not conceptualized abstractly. But they approach the language of definition, so far as they are cast in the present tense; these are things man *always* does. But expression of the definitive word "always" is absent.

The same generic present of the activist verb partly prevails in Hesiod's previous topicalization. There is a difference between this generalized usage and the same tense as it occurs in narrative to index action going on *now* before one's eye—not necessarily "going on always." Once the use of "topics" for discourse became an accepted habit, pressure mounted for predicates which after first supplying an "always action" could convert this into an "always condition," that is, relationship. Static "facts of the case" began to replace dynamic "goings on." In the language of philosophy, "being" (as a form of syntax) began to replace "becoming."

The change is one that still grows out of the ability to read language visually in its alphabetized form instead of hearing it pronounced acoustically. The contrast can be illustrated by quotation from the opening pages of Aristotle's *Politics,* in which we hear a later echo of the same anthropology and which may indeed carry a reminiscence of the Sophoclean chorus, but with a big difference:

> From these [considerations] it is evident that the city is [one] of the things-by-nature, and that man [*anthropos*] by nature [is] a city-animal, and that the non-city man [*apolis,* as in *Antig.* 360] due to nature not some vicissitude is surely either a worthless [person] or a superman—like the one reviled by Homer: "clanless, lawless, heartless" [*anestios:* cf. *mete emoi parestios* in *Antig.* 372]. . . . Man alone of animals possesses discourse. . . . As man is best of the animals [*beltison zōion*], so also sundered from law and justice he [is] worst of all.
>
> [Cf. *Antigone* 332–33: *polla ta deina kai ouden anthropou deinoteron.*]

A sentiment shared by both contexts, one of the mid-fifth century, the other of the late fourth, is nevertheless expressed in two quite different modes of syntax. Both share "man" as a general name, not that of a specific person like an "Achilles" or an "Odysseus" which had been the typical idiom of memorized orality. But by the time the Aristotelean passage was written, it had become possible to describe this "man" not by narrating what he does, but by linking "him" as a "subject" to a series of predicates connoting something fixed, something that is an object of thought: the predicate describes a class, or a property, not an action. In the idiom suitable for this purpose the verb "to be" is used to signify not a "presence" or a "forceful existence" (its common use in oralism) but a mere linkage required by a conceptual operation. The narrativized usage has turned into a logical one. This conceptual idiom also requires that

Greek predicates become generalized, using the generic neuter (that is, the non-gender, the non-personal), as in "the [things] by nature ... best of animals ... worst of animals" (not "best animal ... worst animal"). This use of the generic neuter occurs in a few Homeric maxims but (so far as I know) is confined to them. In oralism it does not become an idiom of discursive speech. Sophocles uses it to introduce the *Antigone* chorus ("the formidable [things] are many, and no [thing] more formidable"), but he then drops it. It is comparatively rare in tragedy, as in Homer. In philosophy, on the other hand, conceptual force was being assisted by this usage, especially as applied to the Greek definite article (Snell 1924).

It is not artificial to charge these conceptual advances in idiom to the account of the written alphabet. The standard explanation of such a difference between two "authors" resorts to the truism that the two were of different professions, one a poet, the other a philosopher, and that their vocabulary differs accordingly. This presumes that the two professions with their corresponding idioms were both available to Greeks of the fifth century and that a Sophocles was an author who happened to choose one rather than the other, in the manner of his modern counterparts. The testimony of the vocabulary contained in the texts we have, from Homer to Euripides, tells against this conclusion. The alternative explanation is that the idiom represents something that had slowly become possible only as the pressure to compose discourse for oral memorization had been lifted by the introduction of an alternative means. The composer, seeking survival for what he was composing, found that the artifact he was creating could do this for him by simply existing as an artifact.

The substitution of the "timeless present," turning into the "logical present," in place of the "immediate present" or the past or future, became a preoccupation of the pre-Platonic philosophers, particularly Parmenides. His verse indeed vividly illustrates the dynamics of the partnership between oral and written idiom as they existed in his day. This is no place to examine his system, except to note his dramatization of the verb "to be" in its present tense *esti* and its neuter generic present participle *eon* as embodying a linguistic usage which, as he saw it, must replace the Homeric language of action and event—of "becoming" and "perishing." Discussion of the logical and epistemological and ontological dimensions of this verb has become a commonplace among historians of Greek thought, especially as such concerns come to the fore in Plato's dialogues, which, it must always be remembered, were written documents, the fruit of a writer's lifetime preoccupation. Sufficient here to say that the genesis of this Greek problem becomes uncovered once it is placed in the context supplied by the special theory of Greek literacy.

Could the Muse learn, if not to sing, at least to write, in the verb "to be" rather than in the verb "to do"? One genre of composition shared by the muse of Homer and the muse of Alexandria was the "hymn" celebrating the status and functions of a given deity. The Homeric "author" of a hymn to Aphrodite proceeds to indicate her unusual parentage and then some specifics of her character by a narrative short story. She is mistress of Cyprus

> whither the humid force of blowing zephyr carried her
> over the wave of the foam-roaring sea within mollient
> foam. And her the seasons received welcoming and put
> ambrosial garments around her and on her immortal
> head they set a well-fashioned crown [both] beautiful
> [and] golden . . . and when they had put the adornment
> entire upon her [body's] flesh, they brought her into
> [the company of] the immortals.
>
> [*Homeric Hymn* VI, ll. 3–15]

The passage, like the rest of the hymn that follows it, illustrates standard oralist technique for "drawing a portrait" as we would say. Only, this is not a still-life portrait, but a piece of cinema: a beautiful woman emerging from sea foam is wafted ashore and is then dressed in her boudoir by her attendants before being introduced to the waiting company in a formal reception. The language evokes tactile mobility—the softness of the foam-bed, the warm wetness of the wind, the caressed surface of a woman's body.

Similarly, Callimachus celebrates Zeus by first addressing the circumstance of parentage:

> In Parrhasia it was that Rhea bare you, where was a hill sheltered with thickest brush. Thence is the place holy. . . . There when your mother had laid you down from her mighty lap, straightway she sought a stream of water, wherewith she might purge her of the soilure of birth and wash your body therein. But mighty Ladon flowed not yet, nor Erymanthus clearest of rivers; waterless was all Arcadia, yet was it anon to be called wellwatered. For at that time when Rhea loosed her girdle, full many a hollow oak did watery Ladon bear aloft, and many a wain did Melas carry and many a serpent above Carnion, wet though it now be, cast its lair. . . ."
>
> [Callimachus, *Hymn to Zeus*, ll. 10–25; Loeb translation]

In this poetry written for literate readers the narrative syntax of oralism still survives: "When your mother laid you down . . . she sought a stream. . . ." (Even so, oralism would more likely have avoided the subordinate clause, saying instead, paratactically, "she laid you down and sought a stream.") But clearly the overall syntax is quite different. Explanation of the contrast between the two styles normally attaches itself to what is obvious—the increased weight of learned allusion, which burdens the verse in accordance with the conventions of scholarly poetry. But the difference goes deeper: the narrative syntax of memorizable oralism has been invaded by the static syntax of literate description: "where *was* a hill . . . thence *is* the place holy . . . Ladon flowed not yet . . . waterless *was* all Arcadia

. . . yet *was it* [the verb *mellein* used of historical fact] anon to be called well-watered . . . wet though it *now be.* . . ."

Though past tenses intermingle with present, they are not the past of actions performed in memorized narrative, but the past of historic fact, which now exists fixed in the mind of the present. The verb "to be," linking a subject and its property in a timeless connection, intrudes as it never could in oralist language. This is not cinema, but still life, a writer's portraiture. But yet, is it not poetry? The Muse has learnt to put her song into writing and in doing so tries to sing in the language of Aristotle.

Has Greek discourse—the contrived and cunning word—as it passes out of orality into literacy, started to devalue itself? Here are competing versions of the human experience, of what is perceived as a human reality. The one narrates an occasion which is dramatized, the other places the same kind of occasion in a historical context. Leaving aside the personalities involved (since the charms of Venus, which give her an advantage over Jove, are only contingent to the main issue), to which of these two idioms of discourse is instinctive preference likely to be given?

Yet there is another side to the coin. Alphabetized speech offered its own forms of freedom, even of excitement. Oralism had favored the traditional and the familiar, both in content and style. The need to conserve in memory required that the content of memory be economical. You added to it only cautiously, slowly, and often with the loss of previous material to make room for addition in what was a drastically limited capacity. Oral information was packaged tightly (to use an anachronistic metaphor).

The resources of documentation were by contrast wide open, at least in theory, disclosing two related possibilities. The warehouse of storage, no longer acoustic but visibly material, was extendible, and also the documented contents need no longer relate only what was already familiar and so easy of recollection. Alphabetized speech, given its ready fluency of recognition, now allowed of novel language and of novel statement (should individual minds be tempted to indulge in such) which a reader scanning as he read could recognize at leisure and "take in" and "think over." Under acoustic conditions, this was not a possible operation. He could also respond with a commentary of his own which might be novel.

The loss of constraint previously imposed by rhythm greatly assisted this process. Prose became the vehicle of a whole new universe of fact and of theory. This was a release of mind as well as of language, and it showed up first, where we would expect it, in the creation of "history" as essentially a prosaic enterprise. If the genius of preserved orality had always been narrative, the inclination of the first writers, as they were able to turn preserved speech into prose, would be to choose the familiar narrative mode for this purpose. They boldly set out to describe anything that had "happened" within their own field of attention, concentrating on war in particular, because deeds of war had already been exploited by the bards of orality as the readiest means of attracting and holding audiences. Yet it is significant that they also gave much attention to the *mores*—the *ethos* and *nomos*—of societies both Greek and foreign as though they instinctively recognized the didactic role of preserved speech acting as the instrument of cultural tradition. The Ionians Hecataeus and Herodotus were the pioneers, followed by Thucydides, the first Attic historian.

Gradually, if sparingly, the verb "to be" appears as the copula required for a stated historical "fact" replacing the powerful and mobile "presence" assigned to the personalities of oral narrative. The phrase *potamos megas*—"river big"—expresses an oral vision (and incidentally constitutes a fragment of a hexameter). But *Olenos potamos megas esti*—"Olenos is a big river" (Herodotus)—converts the vision into the likeness of an objective statement (though the preferred predicate is still a symbol of status).

The same opening toward the novel and the nontraditional, as it provoked history, also created philosophy and science. The new language of fact was accompanied by a new language of theory, which relied even more on the resources of the verb "to be."

Aristotle, writing as a philosopher, and asking the question, How did philosophy start, proposed an answer that was in part psychological, resting on the human tendency to pause in wonder at some striking spectacle, and in part sociological, relying on that "surplus value" (to adopt the Marxist formula) accumulated in society which becomes sufficient to support a class of leisured persons, able to pursue speculation "beyond need." The explanation can be interpreted as in part an apology for his own Lyceum, considered as a club of leisured persons who needed the support of their contemporaries to function. The pioneers of the past whom he names in this category lived within a century (or a little more) of the alphabet's invention.

The words he chooses to describe their intellectual enterprise are *theōria* and its verb *theōrein,* both referring to the act of looking at something. The choice may be a better pointer toward the real truth of what had happened. Why choose vision as the metaphor for an intellectual operation, unless guided by the subconscious recognition that the operation had arisen out of viewing the written word rather than just hearing it spoken?

The continuing partnership between orality and literacy, ear and eye, required Plato, writing in the crucial moment of transition from one to the other, to reassert the primacy of speaking and hearing in personal oral response, even as he wrote. The apparently spoken format of his dialogues testifies to the partnership. In one of them—the *Phaedrus*—he even strives to give the oral message priority over the written, though with ambiguous result. But it was the written which had made his own profession possible, and his literary output—the first extensive and coherent body of written speculative thought in the history of mankind—testifies as much. Nevertheless, after the Greeks, the possibilities of novel statement remained partly dormant.

The conversion of an acoustic medium for communication into a visible object used for the same purpose had wide effects which at the time they occurred were accepted unconsciously (with some exceptions); and by and large they have been so accepted ever since. As a result of technological efficiency, the conversion could become total—the only instance of this kind in human history. All language could now be thought of as written language. The text as read came to be regarded as the equivalent of the word as spoken. Since scholars and specialists deal almost exclusively with texts, the assumption has grown up that writing is identical with language—in fact, that writing *is* language, rather than merely a visual artifact designed to trigger the memory of a series of linguistic noises by symbolic association. Non-alphabetic scripts, such as those of China and Japan, are commonly confused with the foreign tongues they are used for, as though the two were inseparable. It is a misconception which tends to block any proposal to alphabetize spoken tongues. The science of linguistics itself commonly treats textualized language as though it were the whole of language.

The confusion is understandable, because it is only as language is written down that it becomes possible to think about it. The acoustic medium, being incapable of visualization, did not achieve recognition as a phenomenon wholly separable from the person who used it. But in the alphabetized document the medium became objectified. There it was, reproduced perfectly in the alphabet, not a partial image but the whole of it, no longer just a function of "me" the speaker but a document with an independent existence.

This existence, as it began to attract attention, invited examination of itself. So emerged, in the speculations of the sophists and Plato, as they wrote about what they were writing, conceptions of how this written thing behaved, of its "parts of speech," its "grammar" (itself a word which defines language as it is written). The term *logos,* richly ambivalent, referring to discourse both as spoken and as written (argument versus treatise) and also to the mental operation (the reasoning power) required to produce it, came into its own, symbolizing the new prosaic and literate discourse (albeit still enjoying a necessary partnership with spoken dialectic). A distinction slowly formed which identified the uttered *epos* of orally preserved speech as something different from *logos* and (to the philosophers) inferior to it. Concomitantly, the feeling for spoken tongue as a stream flowing (as in Hesiod) was replaced by a vision of a fixed row of letters, and the single word as written, separated from the flow of the utterance that contained it, gained recognition as a separate "thing."

There is probably no attestable instance in Greek of the term *logos* as denoting a single "word," though it is often translated as though it did. The first "word for a word" in the early philosophers seems to have been *onoma*—a "name" (Havelock 1982a, p. 289*n*64). They recognized that in the orally preserved speech which they had to use (while striving to correct it) the subjects of significant statements were always persons, with "names," not things or ideas.

As language became separated visually from the person who uttered it, so also the person, the source of the language, came into sharper focus and the concept of selfhood was born. The history of Greek literature is often written as though the concept was already available to Homer and as though it should be taken for granted as a condition of all sophisticated discourse. The early lyric poets of Greece have been interpreted as the voice of an individualism asserting the identities of individual selves, to form a necessary condition of Greek classic culture (Snell 1953, chapter 3; Havelock 1963, p. 211*n*6). This in any strict sense only became true in the time of Plato. Achilles may have had a "self" in our sense of the word, but he was not aware of it, and if he had been, he would not have behaved as a hero of the oralist vocabulary, a speaker of utterances and a doer of deeds.

The "self" was a Socratic discovery or, perhaps we should say, an invention of the Socratic vocabulary (Havelock 1972, pp. 1–18; Claus 1981). The linguistic method used to identify it and examine it was originally oral, so far as Socrates was concerned. Later it was "textualized" as we say by Plato. But though oral, the Socratic dialectic depended upon the previous isolation of language in its written form as something separate from the person who uttered it. The person who used the language but was now separated from it became the "personality" who could now discover its existence. The language so discovered became that level of theoretic discourse denoted by *logos* (Havelock 1984).

Within the logos resided knowledge of what was known, now separated from the personal knower—who could, however, train himself to use it. Simultaneously, a separate cleavage opened up, between this theoretic discourse and the rhythmic narrative of oralism: the philosopher entered the lists against the poets. Both these breaks with tradition were recognized and dramatized in Socrates' own lifetime, when he was nearly fifty and Plato was a child. Neither would have been rendered possible without growing visualization of the tradition, as this had occurred when language was alphabetized.

Aside from the reflexive pronouns (my-self, your-self, himself) the chosen symbol of selfhood became *psyche,* often erroneously rendered as "the soul." The choice betrays an instinctive fidelity, on the part of those who exploited the word, to the continuing partnership between orality and literacy. For here was the symbol of the speechless thoughtless "ghost" of oral epic, able in Greek orality to discourse (and so "think") only after being revived by the warm blood of temporary human life, but now given a new dimension in the guise of the "ghost in me" which as it speaks also thinks and, through the new life of the intellect, achieves the only complete life of man.

Once the reader found himself set free to compose a language of theory, with its abstract subjects and conceptualized predicates, he also realized that he was employing new mental energies of a different quality from those exercised in oralism. Pressure accordingly arose to give this mental operation a separate identity. One can say that the entire Athenian "enlightenment," assigned by historians to the last half of the fifth century B.C., revolved around the discovery of intellectualism, and of the intellect as representing a new level of the human consciousness. The linguistic symptoms of this radical shift away from oralism, which has ever since underlain all European consciousness, occurred in a proliferation of terms, for notions and thoughts and thinking, for knowledge and knowing, for understanding, investigating, research, inquiry. The task set himself by Socrates was to bring this new kind of terminology into close connection with the self and with *psyche* (Havelock 1984, pp. 88–91). For him, the terminology symbolized the level of psychic energy required to realize thought of what was permanently "true," as opposed to what fleetingly happened in the vivid oral panorama.

The linguistic formula in which such intellection expressed itself was par excellence the "is" statement, in preference to the "doing" statement, the one literate, the other oralist, with a corresponding contrast between a "true" mental act of knowing and an oral act of feeling and responding. A static relationship between the "true" statement and its "knower" took the place of a mobile relationship between linguistic sound and its recipient.

Yet always, the later mode, the literate, was realized only as it came out of the earlier, the oral, and as it still remained partner with the oral, at least for the time being. Very few terms of the growing intellectualist vocabulary were coined out of thin air (some that were can be credited to Democritus); Homeric heroes could sense and be aware and reflect and seek. The difference was that such thoughtful activities were directed toward choices of specific actions, or else expressed sensibilities of specific happenings. The same nouns and verbs in the intellectualist vocabulary first were converted into symbols of isolated mental operations and then were placed in contexts where the objects of such verbs and the predicates of such nouns became abstract.

The close partnership was recognized with a degree of poignancy, in a symbolic incident narrated in the most famous of Plato's dialogues, the *Phaedo*. Purporting to relate the master's death, the text in its conclusion is used to dramatize the survival and hence the existence of the master's real "self," the *psyche*. In the prelude, waiting in prison for death, he reports that in the last few days he had turned for recreation to the task of versifying some of Aesop's fables. Up to this point, he remarks, "I had thought that the supreme form of the Muses' art was really philosophy." But as he turns back to versifying, preparing for the end of life, he reverts also to those ways of orality with which he had grown up. His own previous career had exemplified as dramatically as was possible the closeness of the partnership between traditional orality and incipient literacy. His own dialectic depended upon a growing literate vocabulary. Yet he had never written a word himself. Plato's incomparable insight captures a last sense of the partnership precisely at the moment when it was to be dissolved. The orality to which Socrates briefly turned back was to fade away before the presence of its junior but now more powerful partner, just as Socrates must fade away too. By the time it was Plato's turn to leave, in the middle of the fourth century, the Greek Muse had left the whole world of oral discourse and oral "knowing" behind her. She had truly learnt to write, and to write in prose— and even to write in philosophical prose.

11

The Special Theories on Trial

Was there a time when an oral state of mind, as described, of great significance and specifically different from ours, actually existed? Was it one which continued to exist as a pervasive presence in the early masterpieces of Greek literature? Did the mere act of learning to read and write produce the consequences that have been described? We are not aware of them today. Why is it necessary to suppose that they once did occur in Greece?

Antiquity can be viewed only through the lens of modernity. The image which passes through the lens in order to reach our own sensibilities is one that has been manipulated by our choice of focus and lighting. The thesis presented in the previous chapter is revisionist, in the sense that it asks us to adjust a previously held system of ideas which have been used to interpret the Greek cultural achievement.

It addresses itself in particular to a re-reading of the Greek classics, with attention to overtones concealed in their texts. These have continually received scholarly scrutiny, ranging from later antiquity to the present day and, most conspicuously, in the last two hundred years dating from the inception of classical philology as a discipline of the university. Is it likely, one hears the skeptic say, that anything really "new" that can be said about them is either available or discoverable?

Classical scholarship is an art, not a science, and its objectives as they are selected from decade to decade are guided by its choice of the thing it wants to look for. If the choice be the principle of authoritarian government, it writes the history of Caesarism; if the guidelines supplied by Marxism are preferred, it designs an account of Greek class conflict. Since, as literates, we have only very recently woken up to the presence of orality as a contemporary fact in our midst, revived in the electronic media, there need not be surprise if this provokes a new look at what may have been the role of orality in ancient Greece.

This, after all, is the kind of thing that has happened continually in studies of Greek literature conducted in the last fifty years. A general current favoring the study of comparative religions as a serious discipline produces its Greek counterpart in a flood of books on the Greek gods, and their cults, and on rituals of sacrifice and the like. The psychological theories of a Freud are judged to be as applicable to Greek literature as are structuralist theories of a Lévi-Strauss. The imagery of symbolist poetry provokes a search for imagery in Greek drama, and so it goes.

Yet the oralist-literate equation when used in reference to the Greeks appear to be in a different case. Its application has not met with the same friendliness. Noticed by some outside the field of classics who have given it welcome, it appears to encounter resentment on the part of many within the classical establishment who perhaps would prefer to dismiss it as not deserving a serious critique. The lively discussions aroused by the Parry-Lord treatment of formulaic poetry have not gone beyond Homer. The upsurge of interest in oralism and textuality, and the flood of books and articles dealing with these themes, published since 1963, were noted in chapter 3. But few indeed are those in the list who have given attention to the context where it all began, in the Greek story.

No doubt times change, and in due course this situation will find remedy. The chances that the special theories of Greek orality and literacy may stand the test of time can be clarified if one considers some current assumptions which stand in the way of this happening. They fall into two categories: those which make themselves felt generally in disciplines outside the field of classics and those peculiar to the discipline of classics itself.

The special theory of Greek orality presumes that a condition of total nonliteracy need not connote the kind of primitiveness which is often read back into the early history of societies, as for example in the anthropology of Lévy-Bruhl (1910, 1923). It may represent a positive condition of an oralism possessing its own quality of life, simpler no doubt than ours but civilized, with a special capacity for creating an "oral literature" (if the paradox be tolerated) of its own. In contrast, the illiterates who continue to exist in societies where literacy is practiced, either by a few as in the Middle Ages or by a majority as in modern America, are by definition outside the field of the accepted culture and have to be brought into it if possible by education. This social condition of illiteracy is confused with the condition of primary orality, which by analogy is also "put down" in estimation. Greek oral culture before 650 or 700 B.C. is relegated to the status of a Dark Age, or else unhistorically upgraded to meet the literate standard. The prejudice at work here rests on a failure to distinguish between nonliteracy and illiteracy. The former, though a negative, describes a positive social condition, in which communication is managed acoustically but successfully. The latter refers to a failure to communicate under altered conditions. Yet to judge one by the light of the other is commonplace.

A second objection to the theory of primary orality lies in the treatment which it gives to poetry (and which the special theory gives to Greek poetry). Like the first, this objection is rooted in assumptions growing out of our modern literate condition and read backwards. Poetry treated as a repository for cultural information seems to suffer degradation from its superior status as a source of inspiration, imagination, and insight. It seems virtually to be turned back into prose. A standard of social utility, it seems, is improperly imposed upon a use of language which has quite other purposes.

Oral theory replies to this view by arguing that the role of poetry in literate societies, so far from being richer than that of its oral counterpart, is narrower, because literacy, by entrusting the storage function to documented prose, has gradually stripped poetry and the poetic experience of their dominant position in the culture and emptied them of their complexity. In Western culture, and in the twentieth century, this process seems to have completed itself everywhere except in Russia.

The rhythmic language of orality combined the didactic and aesthetic modes in a single art. Its content was formidable and majestic and yet at the same time spellbinding. Each reinforced the effect of the other. The spell acquired serious dignity because of the weight it carried: the didactic weight acquired a charm conferred by the spell. So does the sweep of a great river supply a more powerful image of reality than a tinkling stream. The burden of social responsibility carried by Homer, by Pindar, by Aeschylus, contains the secret of that "grand style" which was noted by Matthew Arnold without the reasons for it being fully understood. Literary treatment of the Greek high classic poets too often applies value judgments appropriate to the reduced role that poetry plays in literacy.

The special theory of Greek literacy also argues that the concept of selfhood and the soul, as now understood, arose at a historical point in time and was inspired by a technological change, as the inscribed language and thought and the person who spoke it became separated from each other, leading to a new focus on the personality of the speaker.

This explanation runs the risk of offending deep emotions grounded in religious faith. Selfhood and the soul, when expressed in Greek, conjure up convictions which in the West have been powerfully reinforced by two thousand years of

Christianity (though it is worth notice that the same conceptions seem to be lacking in the Old Testament). They form a foundation for the belief in individual identity and devotion to personal liberty which is so highly prized in Western democracies.

To propose that the formation of such conceptions was a linguistic event, that they have not always existed, and in particular that high classic Greece got on very well without them, can arouse instinctive resistance and disbelief among critics and scholars otherwise sophisticated in the application of learning to antiquity. Even the Marxist scholar might find such a notion unfamiliar.

Religious feeling aside, there are aspects of the special theory of Greek literacy which could meet with some resistance from modern philosophers. Existentialism can be shown to have some affinities with oralism, and there has been some intermingling of the two, perceptible among French critics and historians. But how can the German idealist tradition, starting with Kant and expressing itself in many later forms, come to terms with the proposition that the intellect of man, as distinct from his other psychic properties, was only "discovered" or at least fully realized as an "existence" at the end of the fifth century B.C. and that this also was in effect a linguistic event? What becomes of the metaphysics of mind, supposedly enjoying a cosmic supremacy over matter, over human history, and over the bodily senses? Does the special theory of literacy merely offer a barren behaviorism to explain our human grasp of eternal realities?

For that matter, can moral philosophy find any comfort in a historical formula which proposes that the language of ethics, of moral principle, of ideal standards of conduct, was a creation of Greek literacy?

Analysts and logicians, who have dominated so much of the philosophic spectrum in England and America, might treat such questions as of no consequence. But their discipline has its own prejudices. It cannot help favoring the presumption that the procedures of logic, so far from being a literate discovery, are rooted in human nature and always have been if only human nature could discipline itself to use them. An oral consciousness operating with ambivalence and not subject to the laws of contradiction cannot, on this view, be a valid consciousness. To be sure, language is taken seriously as a human behavior by both oralists and logicians. Its vocabulary and syntax are explored; its rules of reference analyzed. But if the ability to do this is credited to the effects of a particular historical event—the invention of the Greek alphabet—analytic philosophers who assume the universality of their methods are faced with the choice of either arguing that the technology of the alphabet was not important because such capacities have always existed or else damning and dismissing pre-alphabetic orality as a truly primitive condition of communication that we are fortunate to have left behind.

Within the field of classical learning itself, there are formidable barriers which block the way to a ready acceptance of what the special theories of Greek orality and literacy propose: they are the easier to describe in proportion as they are more narrowly focused.

An important one is grounded in the belief, fostered by Victorian education in the classics and still very much alive, that Greek classical culture is a unified phenomenon with an ideal dimension which is uniform and that the survival of the Greek classics as the basis of a humanist education depends upon maintaining this conception of unity and harmony governing the Greek experience. If Homer is the ideal poet—so goes the assumption powerfully if unconsciously held—and Aeschylus the ideal dramatist and Plato the ideal philosopher, how could such ideal authors ever come into collision or quarrel with each other? When Plato, in his *Republic* and elsewhere, seems to disparage if not reject outright his poetic predecessors, he cannot have meant what he plainly says. Any attempt to take what he says seriously and to look for explanation in a transformation of values that was taking place within the classical experience must, it is felt, be profoundly mistaken.

As part and parcel of the deeply grounded attachment to these values as they are perceived to exist in Greek literature and philosophy, there arises a detectable feeling on the part of many classicists that their profession constitutes a kind of mystery religion available to initiates but to be kept from contamination either with other disciplines or with what is vaguely felt to be the materialism or relativism of modernity. The special theories of Greek orality and literacy on the other hand require us to adopt a genetic view of Greek culture, which places it in a sociological dimension. It was a process, not an ideal entity. Its character changed markedly as the technology of communication changed. This may seem to vulgarize the Greek experience, opening it up to inspection from outside by the uninitiated.

There is also the awkward fact—awkward for oralists—that a thesis covering Greek orality and the intimate partnership in which it became involved with literacy can be tested for the most part (though not exclusively) only by a scrutiny of written texts. These have been hoarded, copied, annotated, interpreted in a continuous careful process from late antiquity to the present. This textual exercise has been the meat and bones of classical philology. What wonder then that what may be called the textual bias (Ong 1982) is deeply implanted in the minds of classical scholars? The understanding of classical humanism depends on continued study of the word as it is written, not as it may have hypothetically been spoken. To think otherwise, one hears the scholar argue, is surely to engage in a misbegotten enterprise; the clues to the keys that can unlock the secrets of Hellenism lie with the followers of a Housman, not a Havelock.

The textualist bias of philology has been powerfully reinforced in this century by the three ancillary disciplines of palaeography, epigraphy, and papyrology. Each in its turn has riveted more firmly upon the mind of the scholar an image of the Greek word as it has been inscribed, the image of a prosaic syntax growing ever stronger as inscriptions and papyri multiply while the image of the lost syntax of the word as it had once been enunciated, proclaimed, and sung grows ever weaker.

To be sure, it was Milman Parry's analysis of formulaic and thematic composition in Homer that first thrust the question of orality into Greek scholarship, as it has been taken up by several American scholars and, conspicuously in England, by G. S. Kirk. But even this analysis has suffered from an inhibition which prevents its extension beyond Homer: its reliance on the premise that orality and literacy, the oral word and the written, constitute categories mutually exclusive of each other prevents the formation of any conception of a creative partnership between the two which might have lasted at least to the death of Euripides.

The conviction is unfortunate but understandable, since it has been guided by things that happen to orality in a modern literate context. The Balkan singer, however complete his own illiteracy, lives in a society in which his original didactic function and social importance have long been transferred to a literate elite. If he turns writer, he automatically starts to adapt his language to an idiom already available and completely alien to the oral genius. In ancient Greece oral genius faced no such problem, for no writer's idiom as yet existed.

The scholar of classic Hellenism who thinks traditionally about his subject never feels so happy as when he can plant his feet firmly on the Acropolis in the age of Pericles and from this vantage point survey with satisfaction the Greek world beyond Athens. Whatever this world may have contributed to the sum total of Hellenism—and the contribution was surely considerable—its importance is perceived as marginal and its status inferior, compared with the place where he is standing. One goes up to the Parthenon as to the Temple in Jerusalem. Indeed in this era of waning faith there may arise a suspicion that the classic icon is offered as a necessary replacement for the Hebrew (Jenkyns 1980; Turner 1981).

Athenocentrism as a habit of thought constitutes one more barrier to a belief in the validity of the oral-literate equation as it is applied to explain Greek cultural history. The special theory of Greek literacy begins by recognizing that the necessary conditions for the creation of literacy arose first in Ionia, not Athens. That is where Greek literature in its textual form was born and thrived (the idiom of Hesiod is not Attic, still less Boeotian, but Ionic), until it was succeeded by Greek prose, also Ionic, as Greeks overseas slowly learned to write and read.

In contrast, progress in these matters in Attica and Athens was subject to a time-lag, not completely overcome until the last third of the fifth century. Persian conquest and destruction in western Anatolia following the failure of the Ionian revolt has made it easier for modern scholarship to grant Athens a virtual monopoly over Greek history. After all, this was the city which at Salamis reversed the naval verdict rendered at Lade, a fact which her orators and poets justifiably made the most of. What had been "over there" was now for the most part lost, and the later loss of the Alexandrian texts of the early Ionic poets has only compounded the obscurity which veils a dynamic period in the cultural history of Greece.

Yet it is unwise to ignore the reaction of Athens herself to the fall of Miletus, the metropolis of Ionia and (one may infer) of the islands also. It was a disaster which had struck at what was then the heart of the Hellenism of the Archaic Age (Hanfmann 1953, p. 23). Fortunately for Athens, she had already for a century been welcoming Ionian immigrants from the Anatolian seaboard and the islands (a reversal of the original movement).

In the field of art history, Athenocentrism has recently been recognized and questioned (Morris 1984, p. 18) mainly in order to correct a view which assigned Athens a continuing cultural leadership during the seventh century as against Aegina (and perhaps Corinth). There is also a growing acknowledgment that a sizable proportion of the art of archaic Attica in the sixth and early fifth centuries reflects the work of immigrant sculptors and artists from the islands (cf. Ridgway 1977, pp. 32, 38, 46, 64–65, 88, 99, 287, 288). With them came the Ionian poets who kindled the Athenian renaissance at the "court" of Pisistratus and his sons. Only then does the gift of the alphabet become a perceptible influence on the Attic mainland among mainlanders. It appears first as the instrument of Attic speech in the poems of Solon, but it still has a distance to travel before the idiom of a Pindar can yield to the art of a Plato.

The expression "time-lag" can mislead if it is associated with the notion of a supposed cultural immaturity in the Athens of Pisistratus and Aeschylus. It is a profound mistake to measure Greek "literary" accomplishment in terms of the standards assumed for modern literacy. The habit of doing so is bound to stand in the way of accepting or understanding that cultural formula expressed in the oral-literate equation. It was precisely this fortunate time-lag which brought about the conditions of composition necessary for the creation of Greek drama (Segal 1986) in all its unique dynamism of language and force of social application. The partnership between ear and eye was unique, and has remained so to this day.

To undertake a consideration of it in all its complexity requires one to penetrate into an antique experience which now lies beyond the range of any contemporary parallel. One plays the part of an Odysseus voyaging to a far country, until perchance he comes back home recognizable and renewed.

Bibliography

Alter, Robert.
   1985   The Poetry of the Bible. *New Republic*, September 30, 1985.
Andrewes, A.
   1971   *The Greeks*. New York: Knopf.
Austin, J. L.
   1961   *Philosophical Papers*. Oxford: Clarendon.
Balogh, Josef.
   1926   "Voces Paginarum": Beiträge zur Geschichte des lauten Lesens
           und Schreibens. *Philologus* 82:84–109, 202–40.
Bernal Diaz del Castillo.
   1983   [1517–1575] *Historia verdadera de la conquista de la Nueva Es-
           pana*. Mexico: Editorial Patria.
Chadwick, H. M. and N. K.
   1932–   *The Growth of Literature*. 3 vols. Cambridge: Cambridge Uni-
   1940   versity Press.
Chaytor, H. J.
   1945   *From Script to Print: An Introduction to Medieval Literature*. Cam-
           bridge: Cambridge University Press.
Cherniss, Harold F.
   1935   *Aristotle's Criticism of Presocratic Philosophy*. Baltimore: Johns
           Hopkins University Press.
Clanchy, M. T.
   1979   *From Memory to Written Record: England, 1066–1307*. London:
           Edward Arnold.
Claus, David B.
   1981   *Toward the Soul: An Inquiry into the Meaning of Soul before Plato*.
           New Haven and London: Yale University Press.

Cook, J. M.
  1971   A Painter and His Age. *Mélanges offerts à André Varagnac.* Paris.
Crosby, Ruth.
  1936   Oral Delivery in the Middle Ages. *Speculum* 11:88–110.
Davison, J. A.
  1962   Literature and Literacy in Ancient Greece. *Phoenix* 14, nos. 3 and 4.
Derrida, Jacques.
  1967   *De la Grammatologie.* Paris: Editions de Minuit.
  1976   [Eng. trans.] *Of Grammatology.* Baltimore: Johns Hopkins University Press.
Diringer, David.
  1953   *The Alphabet: A Key to the History of Mankind.* 2nd ed. rev. New York: Philosophical Library.
Eisenstein, Elizabeth.
  1979   *The Printing Press as an Agent of Change: Communications and Cultural Transformations in Early-Modern Europe,* 2 vols. New York: Cambridge University Press.
Febvre, Lucien, and Henri-Jean Martin.
  1958   *L'Apparition du livre.* Paris: Editions Albin-Michel.
Finnegan, Ruth.
  1970   *Oral Literature in Africa.* Oxford: Clarendon Press.
  1982   Oral Literature and Writing in the South Pacific. In *Oral and Traditional Literatures,* ed. N. Simms. *Pacific Quarterly* 7.
Gelb, I. J.
  1952   *A Study of Writing: The Foundations of Grammatology.* Chicago: University of Chicago Press. Rev. ed. 1963.
Goody, Jack.
  1972   The Myth of the Bagre. Oxford
  1977   The Domestication of the Savage Mind. Cambridge: Cambridge University Press.
Goody, Jack, and Ian Watt.
  1968   The Consequences of Literacy. In *Literacy in Traditional Societies,* ed. J. Goody, pp. 27–68. Cambridge: Cambridge University Press.
Goold, G. P.
  1960   Homer and the Alphabet. *TAPA* 91(1960):272–91.
Grene, D.
  1954   *The Complete Greek Tragedies. Sophocles I.* Chicago: University of Chicago Press.

Gulley, Norman.
1964   Homer, Plato and the Two Cultures. *CR* n.s. 14:31–33.
Hanfmann, George M. A.
1953   Ionia, Leader or Follower? *HSCP* 61:1–37.
Harding, D. W.
1968   Review of A. R. Luria, *The Mind of a Mnemonist*. *New York Review of Books*, April 9, pp. 10–12.
Hartman, Geoffrey.
1981   *Saving the Text: Literature/Derrida/Philosophy.* Baltimore: Johns Hopkins University Press.
Havelock, E. A.
1952   Why Was Socrates Tried? In *Studies in Honour of Gilbert Norwood*, Phoenix Suppl. 1:95–109. Toronto: University of Toronto Press.
1957   *The Liberal Temper in Greek Politics.* New Haven: Yale University Press; London: Jonathan Cape.
1958   Parmenides and Odysseus. *HSCP* 63:133–43.
1963   *Preface to Plato.* Cambridge, MA: Harvard University Press; Oxford: Basil Blackwell. Reissued, New York: Grossett and Dunlap, 1967; Harvard University Press, 1971. Italian trans. *Cultura Orale e Civilta della Scrittura.* Rome: Laterza, 1973.
1966a   *Preliteracy and the Presocratics.* Institute of Classical Studies Bulletin No. 13:44–67. University of London.
1966b   Thoughtful Hesiod. *YCS* 20:61–72.
1969   Dikaiosune: An Essay in Greek Intellectual History. *Phoenix* 23:49–70.
1972   The Socratic Self as it is parodied in Aristophanes' *Clouds. YCS* 22:1–18.
1973a   Prologue to Greek Literacy. In *University of Cincinnati Classical Studies II*, pp. 331–91. Oklahoma: University of Oklahoma Press.
1973b   The Sophistication of Homer. In *I. A. Richards: Essays in His Honor*, pp. 259–75. New York: Oxford University Press.
1976   *Origins of Western Literacy.* Toronto: Ontario Institute for Studies in Education. French trans. *Aux origines de la civilisation écrite en Occident.* Paris: Librairie François Maspero, 1981.
1978a   *The Greek Concept of Justice from Its Shadow in Homer to Its Substance in Plato.* Cambridge, MA: Harvard University Press. Italian trans. *Dike: La Nascita della Coscienza.* Rome: Laterza, 1981.

Havelock (cont.).
1978b   The Alphabetisation of Homer. In *Communication Arts in the Ancient World*, ed. Havelock and Hershbell, pp. 3–21. New York: Hastings House.
1979   The Ancient Art of Oral Poetry. *Philosophy and Rhetoric* 12:187–202.
1980   The Oral Composition of Greek Drama. *Quaderni Urbanati di Cultura Classica* 35:61–113.
1981   The Cosmic Myths of Homer and Hesiod. In *Mito, storia e societa: Atti di 3° Congresso internazionale di studi antropologica Siciliani*. Palermo, Sicily (in press).
1982a   *The Literate Revolution in Greece and Its Cultural Consequences.* Princeton: Princeton University Press.
1982b   *Harold A. Innis: A Memoir.* Toronto: Harold Innis Foundation.
1983a   The Socratic Problem: Some Second Thoughts. In *Essays in Ancient Greek Philosophy*, ed. Anton and Preus, 2:147–73. Albany: State University of New York.
1983b   The Linguistic Task of the Presocratics. In *Language and Thought in Early Greek Philosophy*, ed. Kevin Robb, pp. 7–82. La Salle, Illinois: Monist Library of Philosophy.
1984   The Orality of Socrates and the Literacy of Plato. In *New Essays on Socrates*, ed. Eugene Kelly, pp. 67–93. Washington, D.C.: University Press of America.
1985   Oral Composition in the *Oedipus Tyrannus* of Sophocles. *New Literary History* 16:175–97.
Householder, F.
1959   Review of Emmett Bennett and Others. *CJ* 54:379–83.
Innis, Harold.
1951   *The Bias of Communication.* Toronto: University of Toronto Press. Reissued 1971.
Jeffery, L. A.
1961   *The Local Scripts of Archaic Greece.* Oxford: Clarendon Press.
Jenkyns, Richard.
1980   *The Victorians and Ancient Greece.* Cambridge, MA: Harvard University Press.
Jousse, Marcel.
1925   *Le Style oral rhythmique et mnémotechnique chez les Verbo-moteurs.* Paris: G. Beauchesne.
Kelber, Werner.
1983   *The Oral and the Written Gospel.* Philadelphia: Fortress Press.

Kirk, G. S.
1954   *Heraclitus: The Cosmic Fragments.* Cambridge: Cambridge University Press.
1962   *The Songs of Homer.* Cambridge: Cambridge University Press.

Knox, B. W.
1968   Silent Reading in Antiquity. *Greek, Roman and Byzantine Studies* 19:432–35.

Leiman, S. Z.
1976   *The Canonization of Hebrew Scripture.* Hamden, CT: Archon Books, for the Connecticut Academy of Arts and Sciences.

Lesky, Albin.
1966   *A History of Greek Literature.* London: Methuen.

Lévi-Strauss, Claude.
1958   *Anthropologie Structurale.* Paris: Plon.
1962   *La Pensée Sauvage.* Paris: Plon.
1964–   *Mythologiques* I, II, III. Paris: Plon.
1966

Lévy-Bruhl, Lucien.
1910   *Les Fonctions mentales dans les sociétés inférieures.* Paris: Alcan.
1923   *Primitive Mentality* (tr. L. A. Clare). New York: Macmillan.

Lord, Albert.
1960   *A Singer of Tales.* Cambridge, MA: Harvard University Press.

Luria, A. R.
1968   *The Mind of a Mnemonist.* New York: Basic Books.
1976   *Cognitive Development: Its Cultural and Social Foundations,* ed. Michael Cole, trans. Martin Lopez-Morillas and Lynn Solotaroff from the original Russian (1974). Cambridge, MA, and London: Harvard University Press.

Malinowski, Bronislaw.
1923   The Problem of Meaning in Primitive Language. In *The Meaning of Meaning,* ed. Ogden and Richards. New York: Harcourt Brace; London: Kegan Paul Trench Trubner.

Mayr, Ernst.
1963   *Animal Species and Evolution.* Cambridge, MA: Belknap Press of Harvard University Press.

McDiarmid, John.
1953   Theophrastus on the Presocratic Causes. *HSCP* 61:85–156.

McLuhan, Marshall.
1962   *The Gutenberg Galaxy: The Making of Typographic Man.* Toronto: University of Toronto Press.

MacQuarrie, John.
    1985   Clearing the Mists from Olympus. *New York Times Book Review,*
             October 6.
Morris, Sarah P.
    1984   *The Black and White Style: Athens and Aigina in the Orientalizing
             Period.* New Haven and London: Yale University Press.
Nilsson, Martin P.
    1933   *Homer and Mycenae.* London: Methuen. Reprinted, New York:
             Cooper Square Publishers, 1968.
Ong, Walter J.
    1958   *Ramus; Method and the Decay of Dialogue.* Cambridge, MA: Har-
             vard University Press.
    1967   *The Presence of the Word.* New Haven and London: Yale Univer-
             sity Press.
    1971   *Rhetoric, Romance, and Technology.* Ithaca and London: Cornell
             University Press.
    1977   *Interfaces of the Word.* Ithaca and London: Cornell University
             Press.
    1982   *Orality and Literacy.* London and New York: Methuen.
Parry, A. M.
    1966   Have We Homer's *Iliad? YCS* 20:177–216.
    1971   Editor, *The Making of Homeric Verse.* Oxford: Clarendon Press.
Parry, Milman.
    1928   *L'Epithète traditionelle dans Homère.* Paris: Société Editrice des
             Belles Lettres.
    1930   Studies in the Epic Technique of Oral Verse-Making: I. Homer
             and the Homeric Style. *HSCP* 41:73–147.
    1932   Studies in the Epic Technique of Oral Verse-Making: II. The
             Homeric Language as the Language of an Oral Poetry. *HSCP*
             43:1–50.
Pfeiffer, Robert.
    1941   *Introduction to the Old Testament.* 2nd ed. New York: Harper.
    1957   *The Hebrew Iliad,* trans. from the original Hebrew with general
             and chapter introductions by William G. Pollard. New York:
             Harper and Brothers.
Pollard, W. G.
    1957   *The Hebrew Iliad* (see Pfeiffer, above).
Ridgway, Brunilde S.
    1977   *The Archaic Style in Greek Sculpture.* Princeton: Princeton Uni-
             versity Press.

Ritter, H., and L. Preller.
1913   Historia Philosophiae Graecae; testimonia auctorum conlege-
         runt notisque instruxerunt. Gotha (10th ed., 1934).
Robb, Kevin.
1978   The Poetic Sources of the Greek Alphabet: Rhythm and Abe-
         cedarium from Phoenician to Greek. In *Communication Arts in
         the Ancient World*, pp. 23–36. New York: Hastings House.
1983   Editor, *Language and Thought in Early Greek Philosophy*. LaSalle,
         Illinois: Monist Library of Philosophy.
Rousseau, Jean-Jacques.
1762   *Essai sur l'origine des langues: ou il est parlé de la mélodie et de
         l'imitation musicale*. Reprinted in *Oeuvres* (21 vols., 1820–23),
         13:143–221. Paris: E A Lequien.
Segal, Charles.
1986   Tragedy, Orality, Literacy. In *Oralita: Cultura, Letteratura, Dis-
         corso: Atti del Convegno Internazionale a cura di Bruno Gentili e
         Giuseppe Paioni*. Rome: Edizioni dell' Ateneo.
Snell, Bruno.
1924   Die Ausdrücke für den Begriff des Wissens in der vor-
         Platonischen Philosophie. *Philol. Untersuch.* 29, Berlin.
1953   *The Discovery of Mind* (tr. T. Rosenmeyer). Oxford: Oxford Uni-
         versity Press.
Stewart, Zeph.
1958   Democritus and the Cynics. *HSCP* 63:179–91.
Tedlock, D.
1977   Toward an Oral Poetics. *New Literary History* 8:507–19.
Turner, Frank M.
1981   *The Greek Heritage in Victorian Britain*. New Haven and London:
         Yale University Press.
Vernant, J.-P.
1967   Tensions and Ambiguities in Greek Tragedy. In *Interpretation:
         Theory and Practice*, ed. C. A. Singleton, Baltimore: Johns
         Hopkins University Press.
Wade-Gery, H. T.
1952   *The Poet of the Iliad*. Cambridge: Cambridge University Press.
Watt, Ian.
1963   Alphabetic Culture and Greek Thought. In *The Consequences of
         Literacy*, by Jack Goody and Ian Watt, pp. 42–54. Comparative
         Studies in Society and History V, no. 3.

West, Martin.
   1966   Hesiod, *Theogony,* edited with Prolegomena and Commentary.
             Oxford: Clarendon Press.
   1978   Hesiod, *Works and Days,* edited with Prolegomena and Com-
             mentary. Oxford: Clarendon Press.
Wolf, F. A.
   1795   *Prolegomena ad Homerum.* Halle (3rd ed. 1884, Halle).

Index

Abdera, 92
Abraham, 48
abstraction, 94, 97, 101, 103, 115, 116
Achilles, 73, 75, 105, 113
acoustic law: in Homer, 12; *v*. vision, 13, 100, 112; in modern media, 30, 33; of primary orality, 65, 119; in language, 71; in echo, 73; biologically programmed, 100
Acropolis, 124
action: memorizable, 75–76; "heroic," "tragic," "sinful," 77
Aeschylus: *Seven Against Thebes*, 14; *Orestia*, 15, 93; *Prometheus Bound*, 80; "grand style," 120; an "ideal" model, 122
Aesop, 116
Africa, 28, 37, 45, 86, 87
agents, 76, 101
agora, 74
Alcidamas, 89
Alexandria, 107, 125
Al Mina, 85
Alphabet: atomic character of, 9; slow adoption of, 12, 86–88,

90; superior to other scripts, 41, 59–61; gift of Prometheus, 80; date of, 82–85; invented by stone cutters, 87; teaching of, 87; source of crisis, 100, 103
Alter, Robert, 72, 73, 76
ambivalences, 60, 61, 96, 113
American Indian, 35, 37, 38, 45
analytic philosophy, 121, 122
Anatolia, 125
Anaxagoras, 92
Andrewes, A., 86
anestios, 105
anthropology: and orality, 16, 17, 23, 44, 86, 119; in Sophocles, 104; in Aristotle, 105
anthrōpos, 103, 104, 105
Antigone, 103, 105, 106
apeiron, 3
aphona, 60
Aphrodite, 107
aphthonga, 60
apolis, 105
Arabia, 41, 42, 61
Aramaic, 41, 47, 49
Arcadia, 108
archaic, 74, 125, 126